PRESENTING

★ ★ ★

LIVING CURIOSITIES

OR

WHAT YOU WILL

LIVING CURIOSITIES

WHAT YOU WILL

MARY VINGOE

PLAYWRIGHTS CANADA PRESS

TORONTO • CANADA

Living Curiosities or What You Will © copyright 2010 Mary Vingoe

PLAYWRIGHTS CANADA PRESS
The Canadian Drama Publisher
215 Spadina Ave., Suite 230, Toronto, ON Canada M5T 2C7
phone 416.703.0013 fax 416.408.3402
orders@playwrightscanada.com • www.playwrightscanada.com

Playwrights Canada Press acknowledges the financial support of the Government of Canada through the Canada Book Fund and the Canada Council for the Arts, and the Province of Ontario through the Ontario Arts Council and the Ontario Media Development Corporation for its publishing activities.

Cover image and interior photos © copyright Thaddeus Holownia
Production Editor and Cover Design: Micheline Courtemanche

Library and Archives Canada Cataloguing in Publication

Vingoe, Mary H. (Mary Helen)
Living curiosities or What you will / Mary Vingoe.

A play.
ISBN 0-88754-908-X.--ISBN 978-0-88754-908-3

I. Title. II. Title: What you will.

PS8593.I55L58 2010   C812'.54   C2010-904063-5

First edition: September 2010
Printed and bound in Canada by Canadian Printco, Scarborough

I would like to dedicate this play to the memory of Phyllis R. Blakeley who was head of the Nova Scotia Public Archives for many years. As a student, I worked at PANS and it was Phyllis who encouraged me to look for dramatic stories in local history and who first introduced me to the story of Anna Swan.

ACKNOWLEDGEMENTS

The playwright wishes to thank Jenny Munday and the PARC Colony, Emma Tibaldo and Playwrights' Workshop Montréal, the Canada Council for the Arts, and the Nova Scotia Department of Tourism, Culture, and Heritage for their help in funding the development of this draft.

INTRODUCTION

Ship's Company Theatre has always been in the business of creating magic. Perched on the edge of the Bay of Fundy in Parrsboro, Nova Scotia, the company takes its name from the ferry, the *Kipawo*, which once criss-crossed the Bay between Wolfville, Kingsport, and Parrsboro. When Michael Fuller and Mary Vingoe first founded the company, plays were produced right on the ship. Indeed, the stage, wings, backstage, dressing rooms, washrooms (unisex ones shared by audience, cast, and crew!), technical booth, and audience were all accommodated on the ship itself.

At that time, with each trip I made to Parrsboro to see a show, I went with a sense of excitement and anticipation—just how would the space be arranged this time? The configuration of stage and audience changed, it seemed, with each production. The sets were always wonderfully surprising and inspiring, often seemingly bringing the audience inside the show with the characters: from feeling the swaying and swells of the ocean with Joshua Slocum on his solo voyage, to experiencing the stifling claustrophobia of the residential school halls in *Sisters*, to watching the sun set over the Bay through Miss Helen's sculpture garden in *Road to Mecca*.

With *Living Curiosities* the experience was once again different, though still magical. The memory of the magic of the production lingers with me still. At the top of the show, we find ourselves in Barnum's American Museum in New York City in 1863, festooned with banners and grotesque portraits of the "exhibits," with the sound of an out-of-tune brass band playing, and we watch as the actors, playing the characters, prepare to present the "curiosities" as they appear in Barnum's museum. Krista Wells became Henry Jackson becoming the Missing Link. Carroll Godsman and Tricia Williams became Lucia and Alphonsia, turning themselves into albinos; Lucky Campbell and Stephen Walsh bound themselves together, becoming Chang and Eng, the Siamese twins joined at the breastbone; Gay Hauser became Madame Clofullia, turning from lady to bearded lady on her revolving chair; and Jeanette White transformed herself into the giantess, Anna Swan. Black actors playing white characters, white actors playing black characters playing albinos, black and white actors playing Chinese Siamese twins, women playing men, a normally sized woman becoming a giant—the audience is immediately introduced to the levels and the contradictions of realities that are the story of the living curiosities who inhabit both Barnum's museum and their backstage personal world as very human curiosities. The suspension of disbelief is immediate and the audience's willingness to participate in it is assumed and assured immediately.

In writing this play, Mary explored the world of the "freaks and geeks" and got inside both Barnum's world and the personal hearts of her characters. Each of the curiosities are revealed as the real living human beings who are entrapped by the roles they play as the exhibits. The individual stories are all moving and even heartbreaking, but it is Anna's story that speaks loudest. She was, essentially, just a young girl from small-town Nova Scotia who simply wanted to be with her family and to be a teacher. She speaks with the innocence of any educated, seventeen-year-old, small-town girl of her time; her sweet voice in sharp contrast to her enormous size. The accident of the genes that made her a giant, combined with the economic circumstances of her family, found her feeling abandoned, alone in a strange world where she was subjected to a wide range of reactions—curiosity, disdain, fear, suspicion. She discovers that she shares that world with a group of people who, each with their own specific experiences, share her humanity and who lack and crave normality as much as she does. On the one hand, she feels very much the alien in this world. On the other hand, she soon realizes that she actually may have found a home here. The innate contradiction of the circumstances of the inmates in Barnum's museum and the restrictions it imposes are in sharp contrast to the freedom that their employment also provides. Alphonsia and Lucia, runaway slaves, have found freedom at the museum, but are also virtually imprisoned by it. Chang and Eng cannot escape each other and so prefer to profit by their entrapment. Henry Jackson seems unable to free himself from the life or from his role as Barnum's watchdog, despite his economic security, and Madame Clofullia is ensnared by her despondency and dependence. Are they better off being part of Barnum's menagerie? Is there ever enough compensation for a lack of freedom? Is it possible to learn to embrace their particular "gifts" and to create the kinds of lives they yearn to have?

In this updated version of the script, Mary has presented these characters within their Barnum world more clearly against the atmosphere of the America of 1863. Outside the world of the museum, the civil war is tearing the country apart. Irish immigrants are being grabbed right off the boats and shipped off to fight the war with promises of regular meals, while political opinion within New York City is deeply divided between the pro- and anti-slavery factions. Against this background, the lives inside the American Museum take on even more poignancy.

Living Curiosities, *Holy Ghosters*, and *The Company Store* (based on the Sheldon Currie story) are Mary Vingoe's three Nova Scotia plays. Written for production at Ship's Company and Mulgrave Road Theatre, all three represent an important contribution to the development of Atlantic Canadian theatre, in particular, theatre in Nova Scotia. As so many of those early scripts produced

by these companies have been lost, I am delighted that Mary decided to revisit *Living Curiosities* and that it is being published for the first time. Anna Swan's story is an important part of the Nova Scotia story, and *Living Curiosities* is an important part of Nova Scotia's theatre story.

Jenny Munday, AD
Playwrights Atlantic Resource Centre

Living Curiosities or What You Will was originally produced at Ship's Company Theatre, Nova Scotia, in 1994, directed by Michael Fuller with the following cast and crew:

PT Barnum	Michael Chiasson
Anna Swan	Jeanette White
Henry Jackson	Krista Wells
Chang	Lucky Campbell
Eng	Stephen Walsh
Madame Clofullia	Gay Hauser
Alphonsia di Lugar	Tricia Williams
Lucia di Lugar	Carroll Godsman
Edwards/Gent	Troy Adams
Jones/Guard	Brian Gutheau
Clara/Lady	Nicole Willigar, Paige Harrison

Stage Management by Johanne Pomrenski
Set Design by Stephen Osler
Costume Design by Jennifer Cooke
Sound Score by Marsha Coffey
Apprentice Stage Management by Sarah Blenkhorn

CHARACTERS

PT BARNUM	late fifties
ANNA Swan	giantess, seventeen, from Nova Scotia
Henry JACKSON	a dwarf, fifties, originally from the South but has been in New York City for thirty years
ALPHONSIA di Lugar	early twenties, from South Carolina
LUCIA di Lugar	early twenties, from South Carolina, better educated than her sister
Josephine CLOFULLIA	bearded lady, mid-thirties, originally Slavic but pretends to be from France
CHANG and ENG	Siamese twins, late forties, originally from China, slight accent, well-educated
GUARD	
JONES	
EDWARDS	
LADIES and GENTS	

PUNCTUATION NOTE

Throughout the script, overlapping dialogue is indicated by the use of a slash (/). When the slash appears in one character's dialogue, it indicates that the next speaker should begin speaking at that point.

ACT ONE

SCENE ONE

On stage are the oversized banners of Barnum's American Museum in New York City, 1863.

Grotesque oil paintings of the curiosities, including ANNA, *Tom Thumb, the Feegee Mermaid, Joyce Heth, Lavinia Warren, Madame* CLOFULLIA, *and* CHANG *and* ENG *hang from the rafters.*

There is an out-of-tune brass band playing as the actors prepare themselves to play "curiosities." LUCIA *and* ALPHONSIA *are black and must make themselves albinos.* ANNA *dons shoe lifts and a wig.* CHANG *and* ENG *bind themselves together and* CLOFULLIA *sticks on her beard. Henry* JACKSON *alters his face with putty and makeup. Gradually, they take their positions in the gallery.*

Henry JACKSON *installs himself in a monkey cage.*

Madame CLOFULLIA *sits on a small revolving pedestal holding a mirror. From the side she appears a beautiful woman with long shining hair. When we catch sight of her face in the glass we see the fine sideburns and long, silky beard. As she revolves she smiles.*

CHANG *and* ENG, *the Siamese twins, are joined at the breastbone, held less than a foot apart, dressed as Chinese aristocrats.* ENG *does fine watercolour, while* CHANG *gargles and scratches his belly.*

LUCIA *and* ALPHONSIA *appear to be Negro albinos. Dressed in taffeta pirouette costumes, they sing, curtsy, and mime little jokes. They have pompoms growing out of their heads as if they were children's toys.*

The main action of the play takes place in 1863 at the American Museum.

> *BARNUM and ANNA speak over the end of the dressing sequence.*
> *They are speaking from the end of the play after the great fire*
> *that destroyed the museum.*

BARNUM   I give the public what it wants before they know they want it. And I know how to handle the curiosities. After all, they are a pretty strange gaggle of geese, not your average dinner-party guests in Hoboken. The idea is to make them as exotic as possible, and keep them that way. Some of them pretend they can't speak English. A lot of our freaks are Negroes or Orientals or at least Slavs, so that way they don't share a lot with the average American, and that makes things, well, easier.

ANNA   I remember seeing cockatoos, parrots, a condor, and two vultures. I remember they were set free to fly over the city.

SCENE TWO

> *Six months earlier. ANNA Swan is brought in to exhibit in*
> *Barnum's American Museum. Remarks like "extraordinary"*
> *and "astounding" are interspersed with cruder comments such*
> *as "wouldn't she be a handful now" and "look at those dugs."*
> *ANNA is frightened and confused. She clutches a poem.*
>
> *ANNA is helped up to her platform by the GUARD. There is*
> *no chair.*

GUARD   Move along now, ladies and gentlemen, let the lady through!

LADY   *(in a whisper)* Heaven help us!

GENT   What a size. Imagine taking that one on!

> *Laughter.*

LADY   Think how much she must spend on a single dress!

ANNA   *(very hesitant, a memorized text)* Since my arrival from the northern climes of British North America—

GENT   *(cutting her off)* What are you wearing under that skirt?
(to LADY) Barnum's a humbug. She's probably on stilts!

LADY   Shh, give her leave to speak!

ANNA   I have found pleasant warmth / amongst—

GENT   What's under the skirt, big lady?

GUARD   Here now, enough of that! Move along now. This way to the Egress!

> *LUCIA di Lugar enters in the background and watches ANNA's discomfort.*

ANNA   I have found pleasant warmth amongst you all, our Yankee / cousins—

GENT   Who you calling a Yankee? Lincoln's got us into this mess of a war. I ain't no Yankee!

LADY   Give over! Let the woman speak!

GENT   I paid my twenty-five cents!

ANNA   A pleasant warmth amongst you all. There is a poem about a Nova Scotian exile that we are fond of back home. It is the story of a great tragedy written by one of your most famous poets, Henry Wadsworth Long / fellow—

GENT   A Boston nigger-lover!

GUARD   Please don't disturb the exhibits, move along now.

GENT   I paid my twenty-five cents!

LADY   Be quiet, sir!

> *ANNA recites Longfellow's "Evangeline" as the disturbance continues.*

ANNA   "This is the forest primeval. The murmuring pines and the hemlocks,
Bearded with moss, and in garments / green—"

GENT   Bearded, I'll say, just like the bearded lady! Another hoax!

> *The GUARD grabs GENT and begins to take him off.*

GUARD   That's enough of that!

ANNA   "—indistinct in the twilight,
Stand like Druids of eld, with voices sad and prophetic,
Stand like harpers hoar—"

GENT   Harper's hoar! What about Harpers Ferry? Long live the Confederacy!

GUARD That's enough now! Take your politics outside.

GENT Who do you think you're manhandling here? I am an American citizen!

GUARD No disturbances in the gallery. Mr. Barnum's orders.

GENT We don't need any more northern Negro lovers in New York. Mr. Barnum should send her back to the damn British colonies where she come from!

LADY We don't need your kind here, sir. Slavery is a blot on the bosom of mankind.

GENT See to your own bosom, madam, it's large enough to compete with the giantess.

> *He makes a rude gesture.*

GUARD Come on now, out with you! This way to the Egress!

> *GENT whistles lewdly at ANNA as he is taken out.*
>
> *ANNA is faint.*
>
> *LUCIA di Lugar moves further into the shadows.*

Miss Swan. Mr. Barnum wants to see you in his office. Keep moving, keep moving, ladies and gentlemen. More exhibits in the next gallery. This way to the Egress.

SCENE THREE

> *BARNUM's office.*

BARNUM Well, Miss Swan, we meet at last. This is a real honour. I am sorry I wasn't here to meet you at the train, but I have been off on a curiosity hunt! You've had a little spell, I hear. I am sure it will pass. Make yourself at home.

> *There is no chair for ANNA in the office. She remains standing throughout. BARNUM checks her contract.*

This is still your first day. Smile, Miss Swan. You know, every curiosity in the United States wants to see me, and, well, I try and be accommodating. I like to give everyone a fair chance, but I can't see them all. There are many who would envy you here. I've had some interesting foreign exhibits to be sure:

Chang and Eng from China, the Aztec children from Mexico, the Hungarian minstrels, although someone wrote to tell me they were from Iowa.

All grist to the publicity mill, I assure you, but you, now, you are something new, a genuine Nova Scotian living curiosity!

ANNA   You should know, sir, that my true height is only seven foot ten inches, not the eight foot one inch that has been advertised.

BARNUM   Ah, that's nothing of importance. The average person cannot tell the difference, they are so delighted to finally see you before they are shown the Egress.

> *He chuckles.*

ANNA   Sir, I have received no instruction on what I should be doing, or saying, to the public. What do they want from me?

BARNUM   We are here to entertain the public and to divert them from their own dull lives. Yes indeed, to introduce them to the natural wonders of the world. You could perform little entertainments, we call them levees. Songs, recitations, that kind of thing. I heard you were reciting Longfellow out there; a little sombre perhaps for our patrons. Try Oliver Wendell Holmes, "Have you heard of the wonderful one-hoss shay?" He has a charming lyric or two. You probably haven't heard of him.

ANNA   I attended normal college in Truro, sir; we studied the works of Mr. Holmes, Mr. Shakespeare, and Mr. Emerson—

> *BARNUM cuts her off.*

BARNUM   Huh! Emerson. The man says I am a symbol of all that's wrong with America. Accuses me of puffery and show in the manufacture of public opinion. Good thing few among our patrons read his columns.

ANNA   I shall be returning to the college in Truro as soon as circumstances allow. I am very anxious to return home.

BARNUM   Indeed. Well, excellent then, as a teacher you can perhaps inject some discipline into our unruly crowd. There are many malcontents among them. I am sorry you were rudely treated.

ANNA   It seems Mr. Lincoln is not universally admired.

BARNUM   Lincoln has friends amongst the rural population, ma'am, but
New York's immigrant races don't like this war. They don't
care to lose their lives for Negroes they don't know or care
about. But you don't need to worry yourself about such things,
Miss Swan. You will be safe in the museum. Think of this as
your home. One thousand dollars a month, minus board and
lodging, of course. What will they think of that back home in
Nova Scotia? More money than they've ever heard of; they'd
be happy if their young giantess did a striptease for that, eh?

            ANNA doesn't answer.

            Scots I suppose, your people?

ANNA   From the Orkneys.

BARNUM   I must write away there, see what else they can send me.
Now not to bore you with the business side of things, I have
some papers for you to look at. Your parents have approved
everything, but as you will reach the age of majority while you
are here, I'd like to make it all water-tight. If you'd like to sign
here, you'll find yourself well provided for.

ANNA   This says I must be willing to wear whatever costume the
museum chooses for me!

BARNUM   The public is fickle, Miss Swan. We must always find new
ways to titillate them.

ANNA   But I can't appear in anything indecorous.

BARNUM   This is an upright American establishment. We provide only
the best in family entertainment. I'm sure you need have no
concerns on that score.

ANNA   Sir, it may be that I am not equipped for life here in the
museum. I find the crowds overwhelming. I am not sure how
to conduct myself…

BARNUM   Miss Swan, it is natural for you to be nervous. I am sure it is
a credit to your good breeding in the British colonies, but do
allow me to give you some advice. You mustn't take things
personally; sometimes the crowd can be a little rambunctious,
and you must learn to rise above it. As you do in body, so you
must in spirit. We have all kinds here at Barnum's American

Museum. Some of the finest families in New York are among our patrons, but some are ignorant workers or immigrants who have never seen anything like... a lady of your degree. There will be a period of... acclimatization.

ANNA I would like to go out. See more of the town.

BARNUM Let us get one thing perfectly clear. You must never show yourself outside the museum unless I myself have agreed to it beforehand. I will not have my curiosities available for free. Three things to remember, Miss Swan. One: Never be late to exhibit! It shows disrespect. Two: Don't say anything controversial to the public! I handle all that. Three: No alcohol or barbiturates on the premises! We are an upright family establishment. I am happy to say I have never had a problem with giants in the past, not like the dwarfs and midgets. So I won't expect any with you. You are a splendid curiosity, Miss Swan. Yes, I am sure you will do fine.

ANNA looks at the contract, hesitates.

Your parents are good people, Miss Swan. Good, honest, hardworking people. They will surely appreciate the remittances you will be sending them. We can start at the end of the month if you so wish. It is not easy to raise such a large brood on a little farm on the outskirts of the Empire, but I am sure they are very proud of you. Of course, you can turn around now and go back to Nova Scotia, or join me on my own terms. Take a few moments to think about it. You'll have to excuse me. I've got some white whales arriving from the St. Lawrence River today and now I am told the aquarium tank is leaking. There is always something, isn't there?

ANNA is silent.

BARNUM sees ANNA is still hesitating.

Why, Anna, what would your mother say if you came back now?

ANNA She would be disappointed.

BARNUM Exactly so. Think of your size as a gift from heaven, Miss Swan. You would be very cruel to hide it from the world.

ANNA signs the contract.

Excellent! I hope your room is adequate, Miss Swan. Keep to yourself. It's always better. And remember, the fire escape is not to be used under any circumstances. I'm having a little trouble with the authorities.

SCENE FOUR

The darkened gallery after hours. We hear the calls of exotic birds, monkeys, elephants, lions; the gallery has very high ceilings and a million shadowy nooks and crannies. ANNA is exploring the exhibit cages, now mostly empty, each one marked by a painted banner. "Lucia and Alphonsia di Lugar from Madagascar. Negro sisters born with ice white skin." "The Feegee Mermaid, captured in the Indian Ocean by an illiterate fisherman."

She moves on to a monkey cage that reads "The What Is It?" Suddenly, an elephant bellows, quite close to ANNA.

ANNA, terrified, turns and runs headlong into Madame Josephine CLOFULLIA, the bearded lady. She is serene and glassy-eyed.

ANNA   Ahhhh! *(realizing she has hit someone)* Ahh! What are you?

CLOFULLIA   *Je m'appelle* Josephine Languille Clofullia.

ANNA   *(recovering herself)* I don't… I've seen you before, somewhere, haven't I?

CLOFULLIA   *Est-ce que vous ne parlez pas français, madame? Je m'excuse… une giantess! Incroyable!*

ANNA   *(somewhat haltingly) Je m'appelle* Anna Swan.

CLOFULLIA   Ah, you speak so charmingly! You must not be alarmed. I am the one to be alarmed. I not have seen so large a lady.

ANNA   I am new here. I've just been here a week. I wanted to see more of the gallery. We are not permitted to move around by day.

CLOFULLIA   Ah, it is better to come at night. It is a very, how do you say, "steamy" here in the daytime, with all the bodies which are not washed. Better to come at night.

ANNA   Yes, it's cooler.

CLOFULLIA   If you stand over there by the big pool, you will see the giant creatures in the tank downstairs.

> ANNA *moves to the aquarium tank, which is viewed from above in the gallery. There is light coming from down below.*

ANNA   Why, it's the whales Mr. Barnum spoke of. How beautiful they are!

CLOFULLIA   If you stand up close you can feel their spray when they breathe.

> ANNA *moves in a little and gets sprayed as one of the animals surfaces.*

ANNA   I can feel them, I can feel their breath!

CLOFULLIA   My Clara, she like the whales… she come here many times.

ANNA   Is she your daughter?

CLOFULLIA   She is very, very little, just a child… She is such a beautiful girl, so sweet to her mama, but she likes to run away at night, bad thing. But I always find her. Do you know she sings like a little bird? Where are your parents, mademoiselle? You are very young too, I think.

ANNA   They are at home, in Nova Scotia.

CLOFULLIA   *(mangling the words)* Novah Scoshia. Are they not worried about their child in this place so far from home?

ANNA   The picture of the monkey creature locked in a cage here. He looks human.

CLOFULLIA   The "The What Is It?"

ANNA   The "What… Is It?"

CLOFULLIA   What is it? Is it a man, a monkey, or the missing link between man and zee apes? *(laughs)*

> ANNA *is aghast.*

ANNA   Can such things exist?

CLOFULLIA   You are very lucky, Miss Swan, I believe there are not so many giants as dwarves in the world, and there are so many, many bearded ladies. We are, how do you Eenglish say, "a dime a dozen." That makes you very special to Monsieur Barnum.

Jeanette White as Anna Swan and Krista Wells as Henry Jackson
photo by Thaddeus Holownia

Suddenly CHANG *and* ENG, *the Siamese twins, enter the
gallery.* CHANG *is drunk and searching for more to drink.
He is in the "mad" phase of his drinking.*

CHANG   Well, dear brother, you have outwitted me again. The larder is
         bare and I must go in search of Mr. Jackson to restock it.

ENG   For pity's sake, you have had enough! Your hour is up!

CHANG   Enough, enough, there is never enough!

ENG   I'm shackled to a toad. Listening to you night and day,
         listening to you talk on and on… You've poisoned my life,
         you've ruined it.

CHANG stops, and for the first time sees ANNA.

CHANG	I need a drink. Look at this! The new giantess!
ENG	What does it matter to me?

He sees ANNA.

Oh my! *(recovering)* Good evening, miss. Please excuse us, my brother and I were just passing through—

CHANG	Where did you come from?
CLOFULLIA	*(playing at being the great hostess)* This is Miss Anna Swan, just arrived from Novah Scoshia.
CHANG	Where the hell is that!?
ENG	My brother and I are not familiar with this place. Is it in Russia?
ANNA	Oh no! North of here, one of the British colonies.
CHANG	Goddamn British. Cheap bastards! Still owe us money in London!
ENG	Forgive my brother, he is in the throes of drink.
CHANG	I am just fine. *(He swills the last of his drink and spits.)* I just need to find a decent whiskey.
ENG	Drink, go ahead, drink. You know it makes me sicker than an animal. One day I'll die from one of your drunken bouts.
CHANG	And put us both out of our misery. *(with a drunken dignity)* Miss Swan, it is lovely to make your acquaintance. St. Petersburg is one of my very favourite towns. *Bon voyage!*

CHANG drags ENG out.

ANNA	I have never seen such a thing!
CLOFULLIA	A sad song… a sad song.
ANNA	They are sharing one body.
CLOFULLIA	We must close our ears to hear, Miss Swan, and sing with them…
ANNA	I don't / know—
CLOFULLIA	Here is a place of many miseries we must all sing.

The woolly horse whinnies plaintively.

ANNA	That horse, it looks like someone's stuck sheep's wool all over it.
CLOFULLIA	*(triumphant)* They did! Mr. Barnum's woolly horse, captured in the Rocky Mountains. Do not look so sad, Miss Swan. It is only a poor, how you say, dumb animal.

SCENE FIVE

BARNUM's office. JACKSON is dressed as a footman.

BARNUM	You can close the door, Mr. Jackson.
JACKSON	Sir.
BARNUM	Receipts are up this month. People responding to the cold weather, you know, heading for the indoors.
JACKSON	The c-crowds are b-bigger, sir.
BARNUM	Noticed anything else, Mr. Jackson?
JACKSON	I d-don't know, sir. You mean with the other exhibits?
BARNUM	Isn't that what you're paid for, man, to keep me informed? Have there been any disturbances, anybody disgruntled this week?
JACKSON	Josephine has had a hard week.
BARNUM	Our Madame Clofullia? Why, what has happened?
JACKSON	Someone in the c-crowd, c-called her a man. She was c-crying on stage.
BARNUM	Who was this fellow?
JACKSON	A well-dressed C-Confederate, I'd say. Said he was tired of B-Barnum's humbug, wanted his money b-back.
BARNUM	I see. I may have another lawsuit on my hands.
JACKSON	She c-couldn't stop c-crying for her daughter. They had to take her off.
BARNUM	Damn! Give her some more laudanum. The last thing I need is a bearded lady who weeps. It will stir up too much emotion in the crowd. Is that all?

Michael Chiasson as PT Barnum and Krista Wells as Henry Jackson
photo by Thaddeus Holownia

JACKSON   I think so, sir.

BARNUM   What about the Nova Scotian giantess? It's been a month
           now since she arrived.

JACKSON   I haven't seen much of her. She's most times in her room.

BARNUM   She is a proud creature, but a huge success with the public.
           We will see if she toughens up with time.

JACKSON   Have you thought any more ab-b-bout my proposal, sir?

BARNUM   What's that, Jackson?

JACKSON   I am over fifty years old, Mr. B-Barnum, sir. Sometimes
           I thinks the "What Is It?" has been around long enough.
           Some folks seem to know I'm a man in a fur suit, and some

of the ab-bolitionist c-crowd even take offence. Say it ain't right for a human b-being to dress up like that. I wonder whether it b-be time to retire the act.

BARNUM   Retire the act! Mr. Jackson, in all our long association I have never heard of such a thing. There are always new rubes in from the country who will marvel at the Missing Link, named by Sir Charles Dickens himself on his visit to the museum in 1846.

JACKSON   With all respect, sir, that was near twenty years ago. Times have changed.

BARNUM   I'll be the best judge of the public, Jackson. Are you uncomfortable? Does the suit need repair? Would you like an overhaul on the jungle vista? All these things can be arranged. I am very reasonable, as you know, but let's not talk about retirement. Why, you are still a young man. Why, we are about the same age!

JACKSON   My feet ache something terrible at the end of the d-day, sir.

BARNUM   Well, apes don't sit, Mr. Jackson, so I can't give you a chair. Perhaps we could provide you with a bed of straw or some such thing. The woolly horse has one. Where do apes sleep?

JACKSON   I d-don't know, sir, perhaps they just d-doze off.

BARNUM   Well, don't you doze off, Mr. Jackson. Surrounded by your enemies. *(a little joke)* We don't need sleeping curiosities. Now keep a close eye on the new giantess, and keep her away from the fire escape! I can't get a licence from the city to repair the damn thing! And they say our museum is a fire trap, despite all the taxes I pay.

JACKSON   You d-done wonders, sir, building the place up after the last fire.

BARNUM   It took two years to rebuild the collection! Those damn Sons of Liberty burnt me out for letting Negroes visit the museum. Vigilantes, hooligans, and I haven't had a penny from the authorities in compensation.

JACKSON   Yes sir, they say those city officials just swallow up the money you give 'em and never d-do a day's work. It's a d-disgrace.

Some say you's just looking for a way to get this here museum moved uptown where the classier people live.

BARNUM senses something.

BARNUM Allow me to deal with the civic authorities, Mr. Jackson. Your job is to keep me informed of the goings on with the curiosities. Please see that you do. Your lapel is crooked. Good day.

SCENE SIX

ALPHONSIA and LUCIA's room. It is dimly-lit and smells strongly of mint and lavender. ALPHONSIA is lying down on a settee wearing nothing but a light slip. LUCIA is smoking a cigarette by the window. She wears a loose man's shirt and pants. She has been drinking. There is noise of a riot in the street.

ALPHONSIA What's happening out there?

LUCIA There's a crowd gathering. They've got torches.

ALPHONSIA It scares me, knowing they's out there. Knowing they hate us. I heard there was a hotel set a-fire last month, a darkie hotel. Maybe you should stay in tonight.

LUCIA I'll be fine. Barnum is paying off both sides. We'll be safe.

ALPHONSIA That pretty giantess, have you done spoken to her?

LUCIA Why should I go speak to her?

ALPHONSIA I hear her crying at night.

LUCIA Plug your ears! You ain't got no business listening to her. Leave her be. She ain't one of us.

ALPHONSIA I think she's terrible unhappy here.

LUCIA Who isn't?

ALPHONSIA Why don't you stop by her room tonight, Lu, before you goes out for the evening?

LUCIA Why don't you?

ALPHONSIA If I do, you'll be some jealous.

LUCIA   Don't be ridiculous.

ALPHONSIA   I asked the snake lady once and you embarrassed her so bad she never came back.

LUCIA   I hope she never does. She's a weasel.

> *The noise of the crowd outside intensifies. Bottles are thrown. LUCIA pushes ALPHONSIA back from the window.*

Don't show your face in the window! Stay down.

ALPHONSIA   The weasel lady. Exhibit by day, pickpocket by night. She was good at it. I'll ask her then, Lu, while you're out on your walk?

LUCIA   She won't come.

ALPHONSIA   I don't frighten people like you do, Lucia. I won't be takin' her head off if—

> *There is a knock at the door. ALPHONSIA looks at her sister.*

Come in.

> *ANNA appears. She has dressed in a hurry, visibly frightened.*

ANNA   Hello, I heard noises and shouting in the street. I wasn't sure… I hope I'm not disturbing you… My name is Anna Swan.

LUCIA   We know who you are, Miss Swan.

ANNA   I wasn't sure where to go… Mr. Barnum… You are the sisters I have seen exhibiting, Lucia and Alphonsia di Lugar…

ALPHONSIA   From Madagascar!

LUCIA   Madagascar, South Carolina.

ANNA   Oh I see, not… Africa… *(hesitating at LUCIA's appearance)* I wasn't sure you were really a girl before, in the gallery. I didn't know if it was proper to visit.

ALPHONSIA   *(laughs)* We's is never proper.

ANNA   I didn't mean…

> *The noise of the rioters increases outside the window. ANNA is terrified.*

LUCIA   Barnum's men will look after them. He has more guns than the police force.

ANNA   Why are they out there? What do they want?

LUCIA   Every so often them Sons of Liberty round up all the Negroes they can find on the street, all the ones who don't have shelter.

ANNA   What do they do to them?

LUCIA   Lynch a few and drop the rest off at the outskirts of the city, tell them to go home.

ANNA   Where is their home?

LUCIA   I don't think they rightly have one, Miss Swan, or they wouldn't be on the streets of New York after dark. You don't got no darkie women in Nova Sco-t-i-a, Miss Swan?

ANNA   No… that's / not what I meant—

ALPHONSIA   You talk in your sleep, Miss Swan. We can hear you through the walls.

ANNA   I hope I don't disturb you.

ALPHONSIA   And you talk about something called a ta-ta-ma-goose.

ANNA   Tatamagouche. Tatamagouche. It's a place near where I come from.

LUCIA   You have nightmares. Alphonsia's been to your room at night to see if you was being attacked… I thought at first it was just Josephine on one of her rants.

ANNA   I don't sleep well since I've come here.

ALPHONSIA   Your crying scared us half to death. I almost knocked on your door last night, only you went quiet.

ANNA   You were outside? I am sorry, I didn't know…

The noise outside increases.

ALPHONSIA   Don't be frightened, Miss Swan. Dreams are some important. They say they shows us the character of the soul.

ANNA   I don't remember my dreams.

ALPHONSIA   Dreams are like a passage to another world. Have you done partook of the miracle of second sight?

ANNA   I have heard about those with the gift. My mother always said they were fakes and charlatans.

ALPHONSIA   Lucia, we are called!

LUCIA   I'm not sure Miss Swan is interested. Maybe tonight is / not the time—

ALPHONSIA   Of course, of course she is. We need a little distraction. Put the blindfold on me, Lucia.

ANNA   Please don't go to any trouble for my sake. You have already been kind. Mr. Barnum would probably not approve of my disturbing you.

> *The noise outside increases.*

ALPHONSIA   Don't worry, Miss Swan, you will be safe with us, just stay back from the window.

(to LUCIA) Put the blindfold on. We'll give you a little demonstration, Miss Swan. You prepare to be amazed. Lucia!

> *Somewhat reluctantly, LUCIA pulls a blindfold out of her pocket. She ties it on ALPHONSIA.*

Now this here little demonstration requires that my sister be allowed to take from you a number of personal objects. These here objects carry the aura of your very being, essential in the ability to use second sight. Don't worry, they be coming back to you in good time.

> *ANNA looks at LUCIA, who in turn looks at the bag ANNA has brought with her.*

LUCIA   *(in her "show" voice)* Miss Swan, will you allow me to remove a few items? We must be careful not to indicate to my sister what they are.

> *ANNA slowly nods. LUCIA removes a watch in the form of a brooch. With great aplomb, she dangles it before ALPHONSIA's blindfolded eyes. The rioting outside increases.*

Sister, tell me what I wave before you.

> *ALPHONSIA hesitates.*

ALPHONSIA   A watch! I see before me a beautiful lady's watch!

> *LUCIA takes a sharp intake of breath.*

LUCIA   Can you say surely what it is made of?

Carroll Godsman as Lucia di Lugar and Jeanette White as Anna Swan
photo by Thaddeus Holownia

ALPHONSIA	It shine like the moonlight, yes, I see... I see... It be made of silver.
	ANNA gasps.
ANNA	How does she do it?
	LUCIA removes a brush from ANNA's purse.
LUCIA	And what do I *b*ring before you now? An item every lady needs.
ANNA	Why, I think there is a kind of telepathy here.
ALPHONSIA	What does you bring? A brush, I done see a horsetail brush!

> *LUCIA removes a coin from ANNA's purse.*

LUCIA Can you imagine what this might be?

ALPHONSIA Money, money, it be a piece of money, sure as God do love the world!

> *The noise outside intensifies. ANNA tries to ignore it.*

ANNA I am not sure. Can I try asking a question myself?

> *ANNA draws a newspaper cutting from her purse.*

LUCIA I think we done enough, Miss Swan.

ANNA We have just started. I'm sure there will be no difficulty.

LUCIA She be plum tired and not everyone has the gift.

ANNA Just one more question. Alphonsia, what do I have in my hand?

ALPHONSIA There be storm clouds coming up. I don't see none too clearly.

ANNA *(slowly)* What do I have in my hand?

> *More rioting shouts of "Get the Negroes out!" "No more, Lincoln's war!"*

LUCIA What have we?

ANNA Don't say anything!

> *LUCIA takes the cutting from ANNA and waves it about.*

LUCIA Can you name what I have in front of me?

ANNA Why must you ask her?

ALPHONSIA A number... a notice... Them clouds be liftin'! A newspaper. You be holding a newspaper!

ANNA Yes, but what is the article about? Can you see it?

ALPHONSIA *(guessing)* I see the museum, monkeys... birds... animals...

ANNA Yes, yes! What else?

LUCIA Animals, yes. What in *heaven* is it?

ALPHONSIA What in heaven...

LUCIA   You see the animals, sister, they is hot and thirsty, they's dry as a bone, they's a crying, they's / a whinnying—

ALPHONSIA   Why, Barnum's woolly horse!

ANNA   What in *heaven*! Why, it is all in the way you ask the question. Just like a crossword puzzle.

> *Peals of laughter from* ALPHONSIA *as she removes the blindfold.*

So that is the secret of second sight!

> *Suddenly a brick comes through the window, glass is everywhere.* LUCIA *is still formal.*

LUCIA   You are quick, Miss Swan. Not many have guessed our secret.

> *They stare at the glass.*

ALPHONSIA   But where be your things, Miss Swan? Have they done been stolen?

> ANNA *panics briefly and then looks in the bag; miraculously, the watch, the brush, and the money have all been returned.*

(laughing) So we all be fakes and charlatans now. You gonna celebrate with us now, Miss Swan? With a glass of South Carolina rum?

ANNA   I don't think… I don't think I should / stay.

> ALPHONSIA *begins to pick up the glass.*

ALPHONSIA   I am sorry our chairs is so small. Maybe you could sit down over here on the settee.

ANNA   Thank you. I'm fine standing. I'm used to it. But how do you get the rum? Mr. Barnum has told me, no alcohol on the premises.

LUCIA   Mr. Barnum don't care so much about darkie women, Miss Swan. We can't be expected to behave like ladies.

ALPHONSIA   We also got tea.

LUCIA   You ain't drunk no tea in years!

ALPHONSIA   *(formally)* Unfortunately, my sister was just on her way out.

ANNA   But you can't go out, it's too dangerous!

LUCIA looks at ALPHONSIA and closes the curtain.

LUCIA   They've moved on now. Don't worry, I know where I am going, Miss Swan, and I'm not using the front door.

ALPHONSIA   Lucia… be careful.

LUCIA   *(to her sister)* You be keeping that curtain closed until I get some glass for that window.

ALPHONSIA   Goodbye then, Lucia.

LUCIA exits. After a brief pause ALPHONSIA goes back to cleaning up the glass. She speaks to ANNA through the reflection in the mirror of her looking glass.

ANNA   I've watched you in the gallery. You never seem to be afraid of anyone. It's like you're in a trance, like beautiful underwater creatures no one can touch.

ALPHONSIA   Me and my sister, we been together a long time.

ANNA   I feel like I'm in a cage with people poking sticks at me. I stand there talking about the weather. I'm no better than the poor dumb horse with the sheep's wool stuck all over it.

ALPHONSIA   You feel things too much. I done taught my mind to wander freely. Far from where I am. You should do the same.

ANNA   How do you do that?

ALPHONSIA   I pretend, Miss Swan. I pretend at being an actress in a play. I go look down at myself from up on the ceiling. But you are a powerful woman, Miss Anna. You are so fine-educated, you remind me of… Oh, what was her name? She read a whole Shakespeare play one time out loud; me and Lucia, we hid in the wings. Mrs. Kemble, that's it. I remember the part most with the witches. "All hail Macbeth!" She were so beautiful; she lit up the whole damn stage like a Christmas candle.

ANNA   Where did you see Mrs. Kemble?

ALPHONSIA   Why, right here in the museum, in Mr. Barnum's lecture hall. It's over in the next wing of the building, off Ann Street. He done have some of the finest actors in the world up to the American Museum. Even Mr. Jackson say so.

ANNA   Who is Mr. Jackson?

ALPHONSIA	Why, he be one of our oldest exhibits here at the museum.
ANNA	I have not seen him.
ALPHONSIA	You done too! He be called the Missing Link, named by Mr. Sir Charles Dickens himself.
ANNA	The monkey man!
ALPHONSIA	Mr. Jackson be a Negro dwarf with a cone-shaped skull, a pinhead. Barnum got him years ago, found him in a lunatic asylum. Been with him ever since.
ANNA	But that's terrible, it's so demeaning…
ALPHONSIA	You don't know much about pinheads, Miss Swan. If you did you'd know they's usually so feeble-minded their parents hopes they dies at birth, 'cause if they don't they are going to cause a whole lot of anguish, and for Negroes, of course, it's worse. Mr. Jackson's an exception, he's really smart. Mr. Barnum figured that out and put him to work dressed like a monkey. He's a great actor, better than Mr. Keane they say. Mr. Barnum done pay him well. Even bought him a house in Connecticut.
ANNA	A house! No one has found him out?
ALPHONSIA	Oh, there's them that talks, but they won't prove nothing till he dies and Barnum turns the body over to science. Then he be charging folks to come to the autopsy.
ANNA	He's an impersonator, not an actor really.
ALPHONSIA	Well, he's some good at what he does, don't you think? Probably he be a better actor than anyone here is this entire museum. Why do you have those bad dreams, Miss Anna? Is there something you're not telling us?
ANNA	It seems to be quieter now. I should go.

ALPHONSIA turns back to her mirror.

Thank you. Thank you for the gift of second sight.

ALPHONSIA picks up the blindfold and covers her eyes.

SCENE SEVEN

Second meeting with BARNUM, *the next day.* ANNA *has been summoned.*

BARNUM   Miss Swan, you were found on the fire escape last night. I have given explicit instructions about this. It cannot happen again.

ANNA   I needed air. I have trouble sleeping...

BARNUM   Open a window!

ANNA   But the noise of the city at night— There were rioters!

BARNUM   It is for your own protection I demand you stay inside. The hooligans passed us by last night but next time...

ANNA   And in the mornings there is a brass band playing somewhere and they play so out of tune!

BARNUM   I make a point of hiring some of the city's worst musicians. They play on the street and drive the public into the museum to get away from the noise.

ANNA   Well, it's never quiet here, nor dark neither!

BARNUM   I should say not. I have the city's first calcium floodlights on the roof, attracts the customers like moths.

ANNA   How does one get to the roof?

BARNUM   That is none of your business!

ANNA   Mr. Barnum, I will be forthright. I have spoken with some other exhibits. There is a great need amongst them for education, for improvement.

BARNUM   I am a great believer in education, Miss Swan. As you are aware my mission here at the American Museum is to lift the American public to new levels of taste and understanding of the natural world.

ANNA   So you could not object to some of us attending the plays you put on next door in the lecture hall. I have a great curiosity to see *Uncle Tom's Cabin*. I have heard Little Eva has captured the heart of America.

BARNUM   Indeed she has. Indeed she has.

ANNA	I think it would be of great benefit for Alphonsia di Lugar and her sister Lucia to attend the play. They are so very bright and clever and would enjoy an outing.
BARNUM	Miss Swan, education is a very good thing, we are all in pursuit of it.
ANNA	Yes, I believe you are right.
BARNUM	And I, despite great danger to my establishment and myself, am on record as being firmly behind the abolitionist cause.
ANNA	I am glad to hear it.
BARNUM	But we can only proceed at a modest pace. If we go too fast we will strain our relationship with the museum-going public.
ANNA	I don't follow.
BARNUM	Miss Swan, Negroes are allowed admission to the museum on Tuesday afternoons. This is a great step forward for the abolitionist cause but it is an affront to some of our customers who believe in strict segregation. We don't have performances of *Uncle Tom* on Tuesday afternoons so as to avoid mixing the races. New York society will not accept it.
ANNA	But the Lugar sisters are a top exhibit. White people pay to see them!
BARNUM	They pay to see them on stage, not seated next to them in the audience. Believe me, Miss Swan, it is not the same thing.
ANNA	The play is abolitionist, yet you bar the Negroes from seeing it!
BARNUM	The world is not as simple as in your Nova Scotia home, Anna. People can think they believe a thing and yet not be fully comfortable with the consequences.
ANNA	I think you underestimate the public, sir.
BARNUM	And I think, Miss Swan, that you are a very charming innocent. New York is at the centre of the cotton trade to Europe. Our port depends on the Southern plantations. It is also home to bands of Irish vigilantes who call themselves the Sons of Liberty and who resent the Negro and understandably resist the draft, which sends them to fight in a faraway war no sooner than they have stepped off the boat. Their settled neighbours in New York may find their consciences eased by

seeing *Uncle Tom's Cabin*, but only in the comfort of an all-white audience. Anything more could provoke a riot.

There will be no freaks attending the plays in the lecture hall!

ANNA Am I to be barred as well?

BARNUM Consider it from an audience point of view. If I can attend the lecture hall and behold you for free, why pay the twenty-five cents to see the giantess?

ANNA Indeed.

BARNUM I hope I shall never stand accused of undermining my own properties, Miss Swan. That would see the museum closed within a week and every one of its inhabitants deprived of their livelihood. You are no doubt homesick and that is understandable. If there is anything I can do to make your transition to fame and fortune here in New York more comfortable, just let me know. You will find me a reasonable man. Just keep away from broken windows in future.

SCENE EIGHT

The gallery. Madame CLOFULLIA is circling on her stool. Her reflection moves in and out of the mirror. She looks tired, nervous. JACKSON approaches.

JACKSON What you d-doing here, Josephine? The gallery d-done closed two hours ago. You'd b-better be getting some rest.

CLOFULLIA I cannot get any rest, Mr. Jackson. I don't like going back to my room. My little girl is ashamed of me now. She doesn't want to be with me. She wants me to get the money for her schooling so she can go away.

JACKSON Miss Josephine, I ain't seen little C-Clara in a long time.

CLOFULLIA She's still so little. I am scared to have her go too far. I am frightened she want to go back to the old country... She is all I have here.

CLOFULLIA begins to cry.

JACKSON Now, Miss C, you settle down. Little C-Clara, she's just being a child. She don't mean nothing.

Gay Hauser as Madame Clofullia
photo by Thaddeus Holownia

CLOFULLIA   Do you have some of my medicine there, Mr. Jackson? I think I'm getting awful low.

JACKSON   Why, you had all that I gave you last week!

CLOFULLIA   It was not that much.

JACKSON   It were a whole b-bottle!

CLOFULLIA   It wasn't a very big bottle.

JACKSON   Miss C, I know you trying really hard but too much of that stuff just makes it worse!

CLOFULLIA is suddenly imperious.

CLOFULLIA   Mr. Barnum wants me to have it. You work for him, don't you?

JACKSON   Yes, ma'am, I d-do.

CLOFULLIA   Well, do what you are told then! You black monkey!

SCENE NINE

ALPHONSIA's room. She is alone mending a costume. A large object is covered in sheets. There is a knock. She opens the door. ANNA enters hurriedly.

ALPHONSIA   Did anyone see you?

ANNA   I don't think so. Are you alone?

ALPHONSIA nods.

Well, he won't let us attend the lecture hall. We are not to see *Uncle Tom's Cabin.*

ALPHONSIA   It don't surprise me one little bit. Oh, I done lost a pompom. Now Lucia will be after me.

ANNA   Why do you wear them? They make you look like children.

ALPHONSIA   Lucia says they make us look "innocent." Mr. Barnum don't want us to frighten no one.

ANNA   You are very accommodating.

ALPHONSIA   I been here a good while. Why don't you sit down, Anna? You not on some big stage now.

ANNA   I can't risk— I can only stay a moment.

ALPHONSIA   You don't see nothing. Look, I made you your own chair.

She pulls the sheet off the object underneath. It is a kind of throne made of cushions.

ANNA   Oh my!

ALPHONSIA   Well, sit down for heaven's sake!

ANNA does so gingerly. The throne wavers some but holds. ANNA playfully stands and sits a few times for pure enjoyment.

ANNA   I feel like I am in the hay at home.

ALPHONSIA   You sitting in haystacks where you come from? I thought you was educated!

ANNA   I used to run to the barn and cover myself with hay.

ALPHONSIA   Why you done that?

ANNA   So I could make myself disappear.

ALPHONSIA   I see. Now I knows you don't like rum, but I figure Lucia got some fancy sherry somewhere.

She goes to a cupboard.

We gonna celebrate you finally sitting down…

ANNA   I would stay under for hours, barely breathing…

ALPHONSIA   Just behind there. I can't reach. Can you help, Anna? Right back there.

ANNA reaches into the furthermost recesses of the cupboard.

ANNA   I don't think we should be drinking alcohol. If Mr. Barnum— Is this what you are looking for?

She holds up an odd-shaped jar.

ALPHONSIA   No no, put that back!

She grabs the jar and puts it away.

I meant behind them cups. Lucia always think she be hiding things from me, but I knows her secrets.

Pause.

If we can't see plays, maybe we could put on our own.

ANNA finds the sherry bottle.

ANNA   Put on plays? Who would be in them?

ALPHONSIA   Lucia and I for a start. We be some fine "actors," but no one tell us apart!

ANNA   That can be an advantage, you know, looking alike. It can lead to all kinds of interesting adventures, like Viola and Sebastian.

ALPHONSIA   And who are they, Miss Anna? Friends from Ta-ta-ma-goose?

ANNA   No, silly, characters in a Shakespeare play— I should be going—

ALPHONSIA   The one with the witches, I once saw Mrs. Kemble… "All hail Macbeth" / You ain't had any sherry yet.

ANNA   No, no, another one, about a shipwreck and a set of twins who find themselves in another world where everything looks similar but is completely different.

ALPHONSIA   What happens to them?

ANNA   At first they get into a lot of trouble. The girl Viola dresses like her brother whom she believes to be drowned. She goes to live with the Count Orsino and he sends her to woo the Lady Olivia.

ALPHONSIA   They's sure some complicated stories!

ANNA   It gets worse! The great Lady Olivia falls in love with Viola, believing her to be a man, but Viola is in love with the Count Orsino, who seeks the Lady Olivia's hand.

ALPHONSIA   It sounds like that girl Viola needs a talking to.

ANNA   Everything works out in the end, her brother comes back and they each marry the right person. I should go.

ALPHONSIA   Why don't she just come out and be herself?

ANNA   It's not always that easy. She has a lot to lose.

ALPHONSIA   Who else is there in this here play?

ANNA   In *Twelfth Night*? Lots of people. Lords. Gentlewomen. Fools.

ALPHONSIA   Name some of them.

She touches ANNA's arm.

ANNA   Well, there's Sir Toby and Sir Andrew. They are both knights. One drunk, the other foolish.

ALPHONSIA   Chang and Eng! They looks the same but they's is totally different. Chang drinks like a fish and Eng's a teetotaller. They's always arguing and making up. It would be funny if it weren't so sad. Mr. Eng some unhappy being joined to his brother.

ANNA   Barnum would never let the freaks do real plays, Alphonsia.

ALPHONSIA   Maybe he don't need to know anything about it, maybe we just do it for ourselves, in the evening, after the museum is closed.

ANNA	Barnum knows everything. It's too dangerous, he doesn't even want us to speak to each other.
ALPHONSIA	We can keep a little secret! We go down to the basement at night, beside them aquarium tanks.
ANNA	What a bizarre idea! You're the one dreaming now.
ALPHONSIA	This Shakespeare play done sound like fun. What part would you be acting, Anna?
ANNA	Me? I couldn't play a part. I would be instantly recognized. I mean everyone would know who I was.
ALPHONSIA	Do that matter? Come on, Anna, what part?
ANNA	This is silly.
ALPHONSIA	Anna!
ANNA	All right! If I thought no one would ever know, Olivia.
ALPHONSIA	The great lady who falls in love with the girl?
ANNA	That's right.
ALPHONSIA	Olivia it is then, and maybe I act the girl. Can you read the play for me so I can hear all of it out loud?
ANNA	Lazy girl. You can read it yourself.
ALPHONSIA	You can read the lines for me. Not everybody here have the benefit of your fine Nova Scotian education, Anna.
ANNA	I'm sorry, I / didn't—
ALPHONSIA	I never got to learn reading like Lucia, but I be a quick study all the same… Who else is in this darn play?
ANNA	A melancholy fool, a steward who wishes to marry his mistress, a cunning servant…
ALPHONSIA	You go find this here play for me. I know we got some of those folks right here in the museum. Not a word now, to anyone.

SCENE TEN

BARNUM and JACKSON in BARNUM's office.

BARNUM   I will cut to the chase, Mr. Jackson. Since speaking to you last, the "What Is It" is drawing lower receipts than this time last year. The numbers are way down, in fact. Do you have any thoughts on why this might be? Could it be a lacklustre performance on your part?

JACKSON   I have p-practised the new sequence, sir, the one with the termites and the straw.

BARNUM   There is no doubt, Mr. Jackson, of your having a very fine act. Since Joyce Heth masqueraded as George Washington's one-hundred-and-sixty-one-year-old nurse, I can think of no finer performer of the Negro race who has brought such distinction to the museum. No, I think it is the times that have changed. The ticket sales for *Uncle Tom's Cabin* have gone through the roof. For all those who hate Lincoln and this terrible war, there are those who want to be seen as compassionate liberals and agree with the abolitionist cause. It seems the entire country is obsessed with the line between Negroes and whites, and we must position ourselves accordingly.

JACKSON   Yes, sir, we must.

BARNUM   There is a movement today that says the black man is our equal, albeit uneducated and lacking in all the benefits of white society, but that someday he will stand shoulder to shoulder with us in this great country.

JACKSON   That is something to think about for sure.

BARNUM   The Sons of Liberty aren't having it. What's a law-abiding businessman to do!

JACKSON   Sometimes a place is worth more burned to the ground.

BARNUM   Yes, that's true.

    A pause.

We must somehow keep afloat in all this, Mr. Jackson. We must determine what the public wants and set our standard just ahead of it. Not too far, mind you.

JACKSON   What are you suggesting, sir?

BARNUM   I think we need to reposition you, Mr. Jackson. Let's be daring. Let's put the "What Is It" between acts of *Uncle Tom's Cabin*. That will cause controversy, and controversy is at the heart of publicity. The abolitionists who are outraged by your ape posturing will write long letters to the newspapers, and those letters will sell tickets to all those who want to see what the fuss is about. The Sons of Liberty will be placated that the Negro is still posturing as an ape within the walls of our museum.

JACKSON   How long is the interval to be, sir? Will there be time for the termites?

BARNUM   It will last no longer than half an hour. We want to get them out and home in their beds by ten o'clock. *(a little joke)* This way to the Egress!

JACKSON   The Nova Scotia giantess has ideas for a play, Shakespeare, to be performed by the curiosities. What do you think of that, sir?

BARNUM   Utterly ridiculous! I have made it clear to her that there is to be no intermingling of the races, on stage or off, in this establishment. That is something for which our public is certainly not ready. Apart from that she may amuse herself how she likes. Now let us discuss the entr'acte. We will need some rabid abolitionists in the audience. Outrage sells!

SCENE ELEVEN

We see JACKSON *dressed in his fur suit, looking for mites in his fur, chuckling to himself, and doing tricks with a straw for his audience. The audience howls with laughter.*

We hear ANNA *crying out in her sleep.*

SCENE TWELVE

The rehearsal takes place in the basement of the building in-between the stables and the lower part of the aquarium tanks. It is hot, dark, cramped, and musty. The animals

are in their cages, the whales in their tank. The actors sit about on wooden benches and boxes, waiting for their turn: ALPHONSIA and LUCIA, Madame CLOFULLIA, and CHANG and ENG. JACKSON is hidden in the shadows watching, unseen. This is the first rehearsal.

CLOFULLIA I don't like it down here, it too near the tigers… They not fed as much as they should be.

ENG The poor things have to sit behind bars, staring at their natural prey.

CHANG I'm sure the zebras don't like it either.

ENG And what about these poor sea lions or whatever they are? They look better from upstairs.

LUCIA They are white whales and they are poorly because they are salt-water beasts.

ENG And why can't Barnum find them some salt water?

LUCIA You might well ask why he can't find you a surgeon. And if he finds us / down here—

ANNA gets their attention.

ANNA Thank you all very much for coming. Now you must be wondering what this is all about.

ENG It's damp, the damp doesn't agree with me.

ANNA No, well, Alphonsia here thinks we might enjoy a little entertainment, at Christmastime, something not for money but just for fun.

LUCIA Alphonsia is tempting fate.

CLOFULLIA I know what it is like to be away at Christmas, to be lonely.

She starts to cry quietly.

ANNA Well, this play was originally written for a Christmas celebration for the Queen of England.

CHANG Damned English, still owe us money!

ENG We know!

ANNA Now it will be a bit confusing at first. I'd like to give everyone the chance at a short scene now, just to get our feet wet.

Mr. Chang and Mr. Eng, have you looked at Sir Andrew and Sir Toby? Perhaps we could start there. Miss Lucia, could you be our lookout, make sure no one disturbs us?

LUCIA moves to the shadows.

ENG   My brother and I are no strangers to the stage, Miss Swan. We have performed with the best actors in the world. John Wilkes Booth himself / complimented us.

CHANG   I have the first line.

ENG   It's mine!

CHANG   Get on with it then.

ENG (SIR ANDREW)
     No, faith, I'll not stay a jot longer.

CHANG (SIR TOBY)
     Thy reason, dear venom, give thy reason.

ENG (SIR ANDREW)
     Marry, I saw your niece do more favours to the Count's serving man than ever she bestowed on me; I saw't i' the orchard.

CHANG   Why don't you say "I saw it in the orchard?" That's what he's saying, isn't it? Not "I saw't i' the orchard."

ENG   That, dear brother, is however the way it is written in the text, if you had bothered to look at it. The text…

CHANG   Don't start with me, you nose picker.

ENG   Why, you drunken, filthy…

     There is laughter among the others. This is something they've seen before. ANNA is disappointed.

ANNA   Gentleman, please, we are doing Shakespeare, can we concentrate on the play? Mr. Chang, your character is trying to placate Mr. Eng's character. He needs to keep him on side because he owes him money.

CHANG   My brother owes me more than money!

ANNA   Let Mr. Eng say the lines the way he feels is right and you may do the same.

CHANG (SIR TOBY)
Did she see thee the while, old boy? Tell me that.

ENG (SIR ANDREW)
(miffed) As plain as I see you now.

CHANG (SIR TOBY)
That was a great argument of love in her towards you.

ENG (SIR ANDREW)
'Slight, will you make an ass o' me?

CHANG
(dropping the part) Ass. You call me an ass, you teetotalling / slug.

ENG
No no, it's the play… the / play—

CHANG
I won't be insulted!

ANNA
Thank you. Thank you very much. You both show much promise. Now I think we should move on. Miss Lucia, would you like to step in and read the role of Malvolio?

LUCIA steps forward.

LUCIA
Who will be the lookout, Miss Swan?

ANNA
Perhaps Mr. Eng will volunteer?

ENG
I am ready!

CHANG
Idiot.

LUCIA
I have read the play, Miss Swan, Malvolio is a fool. He be dumb enough to believe his superiors would accept him. I have no such delusions.

ANNA
But you are acting. You must believe in what you say, otherwise the character will fail.

LUCIA
He is a poor fool of a character…

ANNA
But he has a heart, he feels pain. Surely you can identify with that much.

LUCIA
Where be the dignity in trained seals performing ballet?

ALPHONSIA
Lucia, why are you so hateful?

LUCIA	Because you been blinded by this woman. *(to ANNA)* You be asking them to do something that ain't natural for them, no more natural than those whales jumping through hoops.
ANNA	Natural, in this place? You think it is natural for a man to behave like a monkey?
LUCIA	It is what he is naturally taken for.
ANNA	But that is not what he is.
LUCIA	How do you know what he is? I think this be your way of humiliating us. You want to orchestrate this little pageant for the sake of your own vanity, so that you can show off your grand education...
ENG	Perhaps we could rehearse our scene again. I think I have the idea.
ANNA	All right. All right. Let's leave this scene now and move on.

LUCIA sees JACKSON in the shadows. She turns on him.

LUCIA	You, what are you doing here? Did you come to spy on us?
JACKSON	Miss C-Clofullia needs her medicine.

LUCIA grabs JACKSON.

LUCIA	Get out of here! You already too good an actor for the rest of us.

JACKSON breaks free and scurries to the sidelines. ANNA restrains LUCIA, trying to maintain order.

ANNA	Can we please try and maintain order! Madame Clofullia, are you ready to become the Count Orsino?

CLOFULLIA is hesitant and must be encouraged by the others to step forward.

CLOFULLIA	It's not right, Miss Anna. For years the crowd accuse me of being a man, sometimes they even come up and pull at my beard to see if it real... think Barnum stick it on. I would spit on them but I need money. I have a child. I am a woman, now you want me be a man.
ANNA	No, it's a part in a play.
CLOFULLIA	Perhaps if I had more medicine.

ANNA   No, no more now, give it a try.

CLOFULLIA (ORSINO)
            Come hither, boy. If ever thou shalt love,
            In the sweet pangs of it remember me;

            She begins to sob uncontrollably. ANNA *helps her.*

            For such as I am all true lovers are,
            For such as I am—

            She breaks down.

ANNA (ORSINO)
            Unstaid and skittish on all motions / else—

CLOFULLIA   I cannot do this now. The medicine.

            JACKSON *steps forward. He offers her a small bottle and a*
            spoon. She grabs them and takes a dose. LUCIA *steps forward*
            but ANNA *restrains her.*

JACKSON   We are all g-good actors here, Miss Lucia. We all make
            sacrifices.

LUCIA   You stink of corruption. I can smell Barnum on you.

JACKSON   And you is too c-clean, Miss Lucia, you smell like b-bleach!

LUCIA   Why, you little monster!

            LUCIA *grabs for* JACKSON *again, this time bringing him to the*
            ground. They roll on the floor grunting. JACKSON *is stronger*
            than he appears and LUCIA *tears at him.* ALPHONSIA *tries to*
            pull LUCIA *off,* CHANG *and* ENG *stand back.* CLOFULLIA *weeps.*
            ANNA *intervenes.*

ANNA   Stop it. Stop it!

            She throws the book of Shakespeare at them.

ALPHONSIA   Anna, Anna!

ANNA   Of course it's crazy to try and do more with any of you.
            Look at yourselves in the mirror. All you know how to do
            is be freaks. That's all you'll ever know how to do.

            She stops, exhausted, surprised at her own outburst.

            I am sorry, Alphonsia. It was a foolish idea.

After a pause ENG *gingerly picks up the book. Reads.*

ENG "If it be worth stooping for, there it lies in your eye; if not, be it his that finds it." It's very nice, Miss Anna. Very well written.

JACKSON *sniffs. Disengages himself from* LUCIA. CLOFULLIA *sobs.* CHANG *shuffles. No one leaves immediately.*

ALPHONSIA The lamps is fading. It must be past ten o'clock.

ENG Perhaps we can try again tomorrow. We aren't very good actors yet. I, for one, am going to work on my part.

End of Act One.

ACT TWO

SCENE ONE

Christmastime with ALPHONSIA *and* LUCIA.

The girls' room is done up with the Victorian trappings of Christmas, slightly askew, slightly decadent. There is wine and after-dinner sweets in elegant dishes, brandy in elaborate snifters, etc. LUCIA *plays a banjo.*

LUCIA   *(singing)* Silent night. Holy night… All of us can now get tight.

ALPHONSIA   Lucia, stop.

LUCIA   All we sinners so tender and mild. Fearsome creatures far from the Christ child.

ALPHONSIA   You be so sure nothing can change, that nobody can get no better.

LUCIA   That nobody gets any better. Your language gives you away, Alphonsia, you sound like a slave girl from South Carolina.

ALPHONSIA   I never hid what I am. You did that.

LUCIA   So that we could have a life!

ALPHONSIA   You so sure I want this life of yours!

LUCIA   I'm sure my sister is infatuated with a giantess and can't see how ridiculous she looks, let alone the danger.

ALPHONSIA   Danger? You always been the one to live dangerously. You the one to dress up like a man and have a second life. You the one to learn to read and write. You the one to do deals on the street while I work in a laundry. Maybe I's tired of your protection. I don't know, Lucia. All I know is that I felt more alive when we started to rehearse the play. I don't want to stop feeling alive.

LUCIA   Alive. I'm sure you'll feel very alive up to your elbows again in filthy, shitty clothes! Do you want to go back to working in

Carroll Godsman as Lucia di Lugar and Tricia Williams as Alphonsia di Lugar
photo by Thaddeus Holownia

Chung Lee's laundry? We probably wouldn't even get our old jobs back now. The Chinese hate the Negroes. Most of them would like to see us shipped back to Africa. We may be scum here, Alphonsia, but at least they pay us well for it. They won't pay us if we make trouble.

ALPHONSIA   I think you be jealous. I think that's what really bothering you.

LUCIA   I'll tell you what's really bothering me! There's a law that's on the books that says we can be sent back to South Carolina! Doesn't that bother you, sister!?

ALPHONSIA   Barnum's on record as saying he's an abolitionist. He ain't going to allow no fugitive / slave law.

LUCIA	Stop fooling yourself! Barnum will do whatever's necessary to keep in business. This is New York, not Boston. Half our audience hates Negroes. If we make things / difficult—
ALPHONSIA	Anna can imagine another world.
LUCIA	Anna Swan doesn't even know she's a freak! She'd forget you in a heartbeat. I won't let you ruin our lives for the sake of a few fancy lines of poetry.

> *There is a knock.*

ALPHONSIA	Come in.

> *ANNA enters.*

ANNA	Hello.
ALPHONSIA	Hello.
LUCIA	What are you doing here?
ANNA	I've come to apologize.
LUCIA	Apologize?
ANNA	Yes.
LUCIA	What for? Saying that we disgust you? Well, it's true, isn't it? And you, Miss Swan, your four hundred pounds of pale female flesh disgusts us as well.
ALPHONSIA	Lucia, stop it.
LUCIA	I'm just following her example.
ALPHONSIA	Well, you speak for yourself.
LUCIA	We have worked very hard, Miss Swan, to get where we are. This white skin that you see is no simple miracle of nature.
ALPHONSIA	Lucia!
LUCIA	It is the result of years of painful application of skin bleach.
ALPHONSIA	Lucia, we is half-caste.
LUCIA	So what! So are thousands of others. That's not enough to save you. Bleach. That's how we earn ten times as much as we could working in a factory or as a nanny. That's how we can afford brandy and wear silk. Because our mother bleached us! And Alphonsia here, who wants to act Shakespeare heroines like

such a fine lady, screamed and cried out for her to stop it, and sometimes I helped to hold her down because I knew it was worth it. Just like I know this charade of "acting" isn't worth it.

ALPHONSIA   What good is the money, Lucia, if we ain't got no life, if we can't do anything? I'm tired of being a curiosity. I'm tired of being dictated to by that hateful man.

ANNA   But what can he do that is so terrible? Even if he fires you, couldn't you find somebody else to promote you? You are well-known, established attractions.

LUCIA   If he fires us, we won't be on the streets as the Albino sisters from Madagascar. Tell her, Alphonsia, who we are without the bleach. Tell her!

ALPHONSIA   Lucia, stop it!

LUCIA   Mary and Susannah Child, Negresses, runaway slaves. And Barnum knows it. Don't forget to tell her that too. Barnum knows exactly who we are. He even supplies the bleaching agent, through his house "doctor." The same one who provides poor Clofullia with her laudanum and will soon be offering you something to dull your wits and keep you from causing trouble.

ANNA   Mr. Jackson.

LUCIA   Of course, Henry Jackson. Everyone knows he is Barnum's spy. Everyone except you, Anna Swan.

ANNA   He is the strangest creature I have ever seen.

LUCIA   And you don't go changing that with a few fancy words. You know that, Anna. All the teacher's college in the world don't change you. You no different than the rest of us. I've watched you. You never even look in a mirror that shows more than your face. You dress and undress in the dark so you don't have to look at your breasts, of the weight of your stomach, and you think that, if you speak well enough and long enough, the sound of your own voice will drown out the ringing in your ears from the voice you can never forget. Who is it, Anna? What is it that gives you those nightmares that makes you scream out so the whole museum shakes in their beds? What are you trying so darn hard not to hear?

ANNA   I don't know what you're talking about.

ALPHONSIA   Lucia, stop it.

LUCIA   You don't know. You don't know what makes you walk around here like you were five foot three inches tall and dealing with naughty children in a one-room schoolhouse in Nova Scotia! This is a kind of school, Anna Swan, but we ain't no students, we are the lessons, the lessons in what not to be, what to avoid, what to hide away in dark closets, and we are as helpless as the stuffed grizzly bear and the blind eagle hanging from the skylight on the third floor, helpless to stare back at them and hope they don't take you off the shelf in favour of some new oddity. Your brave, enlightened ideas are as ludicrous as the Feegee Mermaid giving elocution lessons. You are ridiculous.

ANNA   I came to apologize for my outburst yesterday. That's all. Maybe the play wasn't such a good idea. I've asked for a room farther away from yours, so I won't disturb you anymore.

ALPHONSIA   That's all right, Anna. You be exhausted, go and get some sleep now.

                ANNA hesitates.

                Go.

                ANNA leaves.

LUCIA   Are you really so in love with her?

ALPHONSIA   Ain't it time you went for your walk?

LUCIA   Anna Swan is a joke.

ALPHONSIA (ANTONIO)
                (to herself) In nature there's no blemish but the mind;
                None can be call'd deform'd but the unkind.

SCENE TWO

                ANNA is alone in her room. She lights two gas lamps and undresses in front of the mirror. It is a long process, with outer- and undergarments. She is completely disgusted by what she sees in the glass and collapses in utter misery. She blows out the light.

SCENE THREE

ANNA tosses fitfully on her divan. The room is in semi-darkness. There is a small knock. No reply. The door opens. A shadowy figure enters and stops a moment, as if reconsidering.

ENG — I don't like to bother you, Miss Anna. I thought I'd try and come and have a word with you. You see, I wondered if you might not give up on us quite so easily.

CHANG — You're wasting your breath. She's asleep.

ENG — I've still got ten minutes in my hour. Be quiet.

CHANG — Oh, for Christ's sake.

ENG — I wanted to let you know how much it meant to me, the effort you put in, and to see if there was anything I could do.

CHANG — Let's go.

ENG — My time's not up yet.

CHANG — Let's go.

His voice wakes ANNA.

ANNA — Ahhh! What? Who is it?

She grabs the blanket around her.

ENG — Miss Anna, it's Eng.

ANNA — Mr. Eng? But what are you doing here?

CHANG takes a swig of whiskey.

CHANG — He has no idea what he's doing here, the simpering idiot. He wants you to hold his hand in the middle of the night.

ENG — Miss Anna, don't give up on the play. We're not trained actors. We need a little more time. Let's not give up so soon.

ANNA — The play? No, that's finished, Mr. Eng. It's out of the question. You saw how upset everyone got.

CHANG — The Negresses have nowhere else to go. For myself, I don't care what Barnum thinks, we could retire any time.

ENG — Retire?

CHANG	We have enough money. You know that. I keep telling you that.
ENG	Aren't you forgetting something? Don't you think you are forgetting something?
ANNA	Please don't shout. Please!
	She gets up and fumbles to light a lamp.
	(to ENG) What is he forgetting?
CHANG	Tell her, you know you're dying to.
ENG	We tried retirement once, Miss Swan, and I concluded that I would rather die any place on earth than alone with my brother.
ANNA	But why?
ENG	Since birth we have been joined this way. Until we were five years old we could barely walk because our faces were held so close together. We have visited the best physicians in the world but not one will undertake to separate us for fear one or both will die under the surgeon's knife.
ANNA	If it's true you're so wealthy, what satisfaction can there be in exhibiting yourselves to the public after all these years?
CHANG	Are you going to tell her?
ENG	You tell her.
CHANG	The satisfaction for my brother is in making me unhappy. There is no greater pleasure for him that that. Eng, I'm hungry, I'm going for some food.
ENG	As you can see, Miss Swan, my brother and I are very unalike, but it is not the kind of disparity that results in attraction.
CHANG	I told you I'm hungry.
ENG	I can't have a simple conversation with a friend or take a walk in the park without him. This drunken devil embarrasses me at every turn, mocks my attempts to make friends, and laughs at my desperate need for solitude. Once I was married, Miss Swan, has he told you that?
CHANG	Oh dear God, not this! Your time is up!

ENG   To a beautiful Irish girl who gave me several children. Her sister was so loyal she agreed to marry Chang, so that they might stay together. Now, you can imagine the delicacy of such an arrangement. We spent alternate weeks at each other's homes. I endeavoured to be as quiet as possible at my brother's house. I furnished myself with a selection of excellent books and in the evening drew a curtain between myself and him that there might be some semblance of privacy for husband and wife. Do you think he would do the same? He drank throughout our meals, even though he knew my wife hated liquor and that it affected my system badly. He told lewd jokes to my wife and made a fool of himself in front of the servants. My life was sheer hell, and in the end my wife could not stand it and she and the children left me. I could hardly blame them. They have been the greatest happiness in my life, Miss Swan. I would think myself the most unfortunate creature in the world were it not for their memory.

CHANG   Their memory! Good God, Anna. Do you really believe all of that? Why, the only reason he met his wife was through me and the only reason she married him was for money. Even at that he made a thorough mess of things. Drove her crazy with his jealousy, always accusing her of giving me special looks, of secretly wanting me and not him.

ENG   That's not true.

CHANG   And as for the reason we came back here, the answer's simple. The South is bankrupt. We were lucky to get back here to the relative comfort of New York. We had quite a plantation, Anna. Two hundred slaves, one thousand acres. *(takes a drink)* But all that changed with the war. Now the Negroes want to be paid and the price of cotton has fallen to nothing. It was time to bail out. But we've made our money again, it's only Eng that keeps us from living a comfortable private life.

ENG   I would rather live a public life where there is no pretence of privacy. At least then I do not feel the loss of these things so keenly. Perhaps you will come to understand what I mean, Miss Anna, if you ever try to go home again, but my brother is worse than a huge body or a deformed face. He is a monster who reminds me that I am a monster. I have learned not to try and be anything else. The play... the play offered a little relief.

ANNA	I'm sorry, Mr. Eng, I didn't know it meant so much to / you.
CHANG	Are you finished?
ENG	Yes.
CHANG	My time then.

He finishes his glass. ENG *is very sick from the alcohol;* CHANG *is only moderately drunk.*

	My brother is too goddamn sensitive. I can't do anything right for him. He says I am too coarse, too stupid, but I'm the one who's made us rich, I'm the one who made the deals, I kept Barnum off our backs, but do I ever get a word of thanks? Never. Sometimes I'd just like to wring his neck. Good night.

CHANG, *physically stronger than* ENG, *yanks him out the door.*

ANNA	Good night.

SCENE FOUR

BARNUM'*s office.*

ANNA	You wanted to see me?
BARNUM	You seem preoccupied of late, Anna. It is just the Christmas season? Thoughts far away with your family?
ANNA	Perhaps I am a little distracted.
BARNUM	Indeed. Sometimes when you exhibit, your mind seems not to be there at all. I've had some members of the public ask if you were a wax model. Now, I'm not paying you good money to have them think that, am I?
ANNA	No, sir, although I hear people pay a lot to see such things at Madame Tussauds in London.
BARNUM	Yes, well, that's not quite the same thing, is it? Those were famous people, great villains or heroines, immortalized in wax. Here people pay to see living curiosities, live freaks.
ANNA	I will try and smile more, Mr. Barnum.
BARNUM	That's all I ask, and a few friendly words. Lord knows you speak well enough when you want to.

ANNA	Thank you.
BARNUM	Your contract is nearly half up. Am I to understand that you will wish to continue your relationship with the American Museum?
ANNA	I had hoped to return home at the end of the year.
BARNUM	There has been a change in your family circumstances then?
ANNA	No... I...
BARNUM	Well, there is still more time to think about it. That is all.

ANNA *begins to exit.*

	There's just one more thing. I've heard a very strange rumour that there has been some sort of ruckus going on in the basement recently. Do you know anything about that?
ANNA	No, I have heard nothing.
BARNUM	Good. In any case it won't be continuing. I'm having the men pump out the whale tank in the New Year and there will be hoses running everywhere.
ANNA	But what about the whales?
BARNUM	The whales are very sickly and not proving to be the attraction I had hoped.
ANNA	Are you just going to leave them to suffocate!
BARNUM	They'll be dispatched and the carcasses will be sold for oil. I have some African elephants coming and they'll need the space.
ANNA	*(losing her composure)* But it's so crowded down there, and overheated! The whales are sick because you should be using salt water, / not fresh...
BARNUM	Are all British colonials such experts on whales? I had not thought you spent so much time with them.
ANNA	They are feeling creatures! Belugas! I have seen them in the waters of the Northumberland Strait. You haul them in here, thousands of miles from their real home, and turn a huge profit on them, and now they are sickening through your own neglect, you abandon them like animals...

BARNUM   They are animals. Or so the experts tell me. In any case,
          the tanks will be drained Thursday night, the sixth, and
          there is nothing more to be said about it. And Miss Swan.
          I understand you have been fraternizing again with those
          albino women. Interracial relationships of any kind are strictly
          forbidden. It is for your own protection. Good day.

SCENE FIVE

ANNA's room. It is late. ALPHONSIA enters.

ALPHONSIA   Anna, your lamp was lit, I heard you moving around.

ANNA   Alphonsia, you shouldn't be here. It's too dangerous.
            Mr. Barnum has posted / guards.

ALPHONSIA   I can't sleep. Lucia's out again.

ANNA   Where does she go?

ALPHONSIA   She meet up with people who are taking Negroes to Canada.
            It's dangerous. I never knows when she goin' to come back…

ANNA   The floodlights keep me awake. At home it was always real
            dark at night. Just stars.

ALPHONSIA   Them stars can make you feel real / small.

ANNA   I have had a letter, from my mother.

            She shows it to ALPHONSIA.

ALPHONSIA   Well now, your mama makes her letters just like you.

ANNA   She taught me to write.

            ALPHONSIA touches the letter with great care.

ALPHONSIA   Would you teach me to write letters… someday?

ANNA   Why, Alphonsia? It would probably just get you in trouble.

ALPHONSIA   You sound like Lucia. What does she say in the letter?
            Have you opened it?

ANNA   I don't need to open it. She will beg me to understand why
            they can't have me at home. Saying how much my brothers
            and sisters miss me. Thanking me for the money. Hoping
            I will stay on with Barnum for just a little longer…

ALPHONSIA   Why are you so angry with her?

ANNA   I just wish she'd tell the truth.

ALPHONSIA   And what's that?

ANNA   That I'm an embarrassment to them, that I don't belong there.

ALPHONSIA   Our mama had eight children, six by her husband, and Lucia and I by a white man, a man who had bought her at an auction.

ANNA   I didn't know... I'm sorry.

ALPHONSIA   You don't need to be. She loved us as much as she could. She decided since we were naturally so pale, she would scrub us as white as snow, if that was the way to get on in the world. I think we must have been a constant reminder of a time she wanted to forget.

ANNA   Alphonsia...

ALPHONSIA   She was happy we got away. Maybe it was the same for your mama.

ANNA   I don't want to talk about her.

ALPHONSIA   Lucia is the oldest. Our daddy had her educated because she was so pretty. But she always said it brought her nothing but trouble. Lucia hides a lot of things and it makes her unhappy. Don't you be like that, Anna. You have to tell somebody. Why don't you tell me?

ANNA   I can't.

ALPHONSIA   You can try, Anna.

ANNA folds and refolds the letter.

ANNA   Mama always told me not to worry, I'd stop growing by Christmas. And each Christmas would pass, and I kept getting bigger and she'd say, "She'll stop by summer." I can hear her telling Mr. Fallis, "She'll stop by summer, make no mistake, Reverend." She'll stop by summer. I always believed her. My father and mother would fight over what should happen to me. By the time I was seven, I was taller than both my parents. My father got lots of offers to exhibit me at local fairs but my mother wouldn't let him. He'd come home and bang his fist

on the table… And then my mother would cry and he'd stop and say he didn't mean it, he didn't know where the money was going to come from, and after they had all gone to bed my mother would get me up and sing to me. I grew so big I couldn't fit through the front door.

That summer I went to sleep in the barn. I didn't play with the other children. They thought I was simple, I was so much bigger than them. I couldn't climb the tree house or ride in the wagon so I just stayed by myself. She always said it didn't matter to her how tall I grew…

ALPHONSIA   Then why are you angry with her?

ANNA   Because it did. It did matter. She got the idea of getting me into normal college by letter, you know, writing my exams and sending them in. I didn't want to go away but she said it wouldn't be for long. She said I would be happy there with so much book learning. Happy! You should have seen their faces when they realized their fine scholarship student from Colchester County was seven foot, ten inches tall!

ALPHONSIA   I'm sure you was a sensation.

ANNA   For a week they just stared at me. There were always boys waiting outside the school yelling insults or throwing stones. The teachers said it wasn't fair to the others. Then the family I boarded with said they couldn't put up with all the curiosity seekers. I had no place to study, no place to be alone, so I fell behind in my grades and they sent me home. I was happy to go home. I ran to the barn after supper and covered myself with hay. Then my father came out.

He said he met a man who said I could make a fortune in New York City if Mr. Barnum took me on. My father told me New York City was a beautiful, exciting place. I said I didn't want to go. It would be like Truro, only worse. I wanted to stay in New Annan with my brothers and sisters. My father said he couldn't afford to keep me. He said all I'd ever be able to be was a freak. I'd never heard that word before. I ran to my mother. I was crying so hard I couldn't see and she held me and said she had to think of the other children. She had to think of their welfare, now that they were growing up. They needed the money I could earn. And she had to protect them. She had to protect them from prying eyes.

ALPHONSIA   Anna.

> *ANNA is crying.*

ANNA   I'm wondering if I dreamt it all, it seems so far away.

ALPHONSIA   Anna, I miss the rehearsing.

ANNA   So do I.

ALPHONSIA   I loved all those beautiful words.

ANNA   So did I.

ALPHONSIA   Will you say some for me?

ANNA (OLIVIA)
> I prithee, tell me what thou think'st of me.

ALPHONSIA (VIOLA)
> *(haltingly)* That you do think you are not what you are.

ANNA (OLIVIA)
> If I think so, I think the same of you.

ALPHONSIA (VIOLA)
> *(laughs)* Then think you right: I am not what I am.

ANNA (OLIVIA)
> I would you were as I would have you be.

> *ALPHONSIA touches her.*

ALPHONSIA (VIOLA)
> Would it be better, madam, than I am? I wish it might, for now I am a fool.

ANNA   "Your fool." You've learned the lines very well, Alphonsia.

> *ALPHONSIA, very slowly, very carefully, kisses ANNA lightly on the lips.*

ALPHONSIA   Your fool…

ANNA   What are you doing?

ALPHONSIA   Kissing you.

ANNA   You mustn't. No one has ever kissed me before, that way.

ALPHONSIA   Then it is time someone did.

ANNA   Aren't you afraid?

ALPHONSIA   Afraid of what, Anna?

She kisses her again.

ANNA   *(after the kiss, very slowly, finding the words)* Alphonsia, you must leave here now. Go now.

ALPHONSIA   I just got here.

ANNA   You're only starved for affection. Nothing can come of this. I am a... a woman.

ALPHONSIA   Yes, why yes, you are.

ANNA   Go now... if Barnum suspects...

ALPHONSIA   Don't worry, Anna. You don't need him. You be a fine attraction in your own right. Why don't you open your mama's letter now?

ANNA hesitates, then opens the letter and reads.

ANNA   Dear Anna,

It has been so long since we heard from you that I fear you cannot be well. Did you get the Christmas presents I sent? I have great news. Papa has found a job in the land-claims office in New Glasgow and we are all to leave for there very soon. The money is very good and regular, so we will be able to bring you home as soon as possible. Everyone asks for you, Anna. Harris will come and fetch you as soon as we can arrange it.

Love,
Mother

PS I heard there might be a job for a schoolteacher in New Glasgow as well. Oh, Anna, wouldn't it be a marvel if they were to consider you!

She looks up.

ALPHONSIA   A marvel... well isn't that something.

SCENE SIX

We hear CLOFULLIA *crying out for Clara in the dark. When the lights come up we see the basement, filled with caged animals. The aquarium tank glows.* CLOFULLIA *is wandering, distraught.* ANNA *enters.* JACKSON *is standing in the shadows, near the woolly horse.*

CLOFULLIA	Clara, Clara. *(sobbing)* Clara!
ANNA	Josephine, what are you doing? What happened to your clothes? Josephine?
CLOFULLIA	No one listen. Clara is gone. She has run away.
ANNA	Josephine, she ran away a long time ago. You are forgetting… You shouldn't be down here.
CLOFULLIA	*(distracted)* She making scenes in gallery. I can't keep her out. She dress herself like grown lady and walk in crowd in front of me, calling me / names.
ANNA	Josephine, that was all a long time / ago.
CLOFULLIA	Every day I catch her in front of mirror, looking for hairs on her face. She is scared of looking like her mother. The doctors say it don't happen. She says she kill herself if it does.
ANNA	Josephine, it's the medicine. It makes you forget; you have to stop taking so much—
CLOFULLIA	*(ignoring her)* She all I have. I am left all alone. She don't want me to come near her. She meet with bad people. She won't go to school. What will happen to her?
ANNA	I don't know.
CLOFULLIA	She is shamed of me. One night she lies on bed with mask on, like monkey. She jump out when I light lamp. She said I hairy ape. You have to talk to her.
ANNA	I won't be here, Josephine. They've asked me to come home.
CLOFULLIA	Home?
ANNA	My father has a job. They can afford to bring me home.
CLOFULLIA	She don't understand, she don't listen. No one listen.

ANNA   Are you listening, Josephine, can you even hear me?

            The woolly horse whinnies.

CLOFULLIA   I need more medicine.

            She remembers JACKSON, *that's why she's here.*

ANNA   No, you have to try.

CLOFULLIA   Try? What you know, Miss Anna? What you know about
            being alone? You go back to your family in Novah Scoshia.

            CLOFULLIA *moves towards the woolly horse.*

ANNA   No… Josephine…

CLOFULLIA   It too bad for Miss Alphonsia you going. She need her
            friends now.

            CLOFULLIA *enters the stall where* JACKSON *waits.* ANNA
            confronts him.

ANNA   Can't you see you are making her sick?

JACKSON   I c-can help her… forget.

            He gives CLOFULLIA *her laudanum, which she drinks.*

ANNA   You are killing her!

JACKSON   We are all d-dying, Miss Anna, some fast, some slow.

            The woolly horse whinnies.

ANNA   She's a dope addict. She lost her child years ago.

            CLOFULLIA *is distressed by these words. She huddles in
            a corner of the stall.*

JACKSON   Mr. B-Barnum's orders.

ANNA   How can you just follow orders like a dog?

JACKSON   I was b-born in an asylum, Miss Swan. They didn't have room
            for me so they k-kept me in the k-kennels. I was four years old
            b-before I knew I wasn't no d-dog. One d-day an inspector
            c-came by and told them they had to move me in with the
            people. Things was much worse there. I was b-beaten and
            k-kicked. I d-don't think about it anymore. Mr. Barnum
            found me, took me out of there. He saved me.

ANNA	Saved you for what?
JACKSON	For a c-career at his American Museum.
ANNA	A career as a monkey!

The horse whinnies.

JACKSON	I work for Mr. B-B-Barnum. I d-do a job. I get paid for it. No one ever paid me b-before. I have a house, money—
ANNA	But they think you're an ape! You're a man! You're a human being! A human being! Can you hear me?

The horse whinnies.

JACKSON	*(fondly to the horse)* I always give him the sugar they give me. Where d-do people get the idea apes like sugar?
ANNA	Are you even listening?
JACKSON	The glue d-dissolves the skin. Each time I d-dress him, I have to use more. The hide is raw.
ANNA	Oh my God.
JACKSON	He d-doesn't complain. I put some medicine in his mash. It helps him forget.

CLOFULLIA stands up, calmer now.

CLOFULLIA	Oh yes, Miss Anna. I hear you go home soon. I'm happy for you. I have to find Clara now. One day we'll be leaving, too.

She drifts off.

JACKSON	The play was an interesting d-distraction, Miss Anna. Maybe you shouldn't give up so easily.

He exits, leaving ANNA alone.

SCENE SEVEN

ANNA enters BARNUM's office.

ANNA	I've had a letter from my parents. They want me to come home.
BARNUM	But do you have an appointment? I don't recall seeing one in the book.

ANNA	I don't need an appointment. I'm going home.
BARNUM	I see. Well, you'll have to be quick. I have some very important visitors this afternoon, bush people from darkest Africa, a chief and two or three of his entourage. I must be there in person to meet them at the train station.
ANNA	What do you want with them?
BARNUM	They'll take over the main auditorium this evening. Huge attraction, probably have to hold them over.
ANNA	But these bushmen, they aren't freaks, are they?
BARNUM	Certainly they don't think so, Miss Swan. No, they most certainly do not think so. Who's to tell them poor buggers? Not many good translators around, unfortunately.
ANNA	In any case, I'll be leaving at the end of the month.
BARNUM	Such short notice, Miss Swan! Your family circumstances have obviously changed. I'm afraid there will be a penalty for breaking your contract. Let me see now.

He rummages through a file drawer.

	Ah yes, the usual, you are to give me half your anticipated gate receipts if you leave before your one-year term is up. That would be about twenty thousand dollars, I suppose. It has to be a lump sum, no instalments.
ANNA	Twenty thousand dollars! Where could I possibly find that much money?
BARNUM	Well, well, where indeed? It would probably be difficult, unless you have hidden resources.
ANNA	But they told me it would only be for a short time, as soon as they got on their feet…
BARNUM	Well, misunderstandings do arise. But these things do happen. And now if you'll excuse me, I have to get to my little bushmen.
ANNA	You can't do this. I'll get a lawyer.
BARNUM	You can get as many lawyers as you wish, but you will find that the contract is ironclad. You mustn't fault your parents. Country people like them often don't know how to read a contract. I'm sure they had no idea what they were signing.

I've had to learn to handle my talent, Anna, and that means minding the fine print. Take my bushmen now. I shall have to be very careful, the last time Indians paid me a visit there was a great to-do. I can tell you, it did not end well.

ANNA Twenty thousand dollars!

BARNUM Let me tell you a story, Anna. A few years before you arrived, I was able, through a considerable outlay of funds, to convince twelve Indian chiefs to visit New York for a stay at the American Museum. You see, Anna, I believe in taking risks, and the public was clamouring to see the wild savages at the time. I had to make the Indians believe that the crowd who paid so generously to see them had come simply to pay their respects. Just as one might flock around the White House to catch a glimpse of a visiting head of state. (*chuckles*) Now, Anna, I know what you're thinking. You're thinking I deceived them. But I know human nature and I can tell you they enjoyed themselves immensely. Like children they clamoured for anything that sparkled, and a great many of the exhibits in the gallery did just that. They would insist on trading a coat or a shirt for some specimen of shell or stone that took their fancy, and at times this could prove quite a costly trade, I assure you.

ANNA Why are you telling me this, what has this got to do with me?

BARNUM It is a lesson, Anna, a lesson in human nature. Something I have studied since a child. Now the most ferocious in the crowd was a wiry little chief known as Yellow Bear. As I exhibited these great warriors on stage, I would introduce each one and when I came to Yellow Bear I would give him a familiar pat on the shoulder, which made him smile, and then I would proceed to tell my patrons how this man was the meanest, most black-hearted rascal in the far West. If only he understood what I was saying he would kill me in a moment, for he was a lying, thieving, treacherous monster who would think no more of scalping a family of women and children than a butcher would of wringing the neck of a chicken. Then I would pat him on the head and he would give a low bow to the audience as if he had just received the highest of praise! Our audiences were delighted at this little deception. But despite all my precautions, the chiefs somehow got wind that

their visitors had paid money to see them. The game was up. They were furious. They threatened my family and me. I had to hire a bodyguard. I lost one of the most profitable exhibits the museum had ever been able to offer.

I think we took in over forty thousand dollars in one week! There now, Anna, you explain that to me, why does the exact same activity become repulsive when done for money?

Human nature is an unpredictable thing. That's why we have contracts whenever possible.

ANNA   To give something freely, to bestow it, is an act of generosity. It is its own reward.

BARNUM   Well, that may be so but you haven't heard the end of the story. About six months later I got a letter. An army officer translating for Yellow Bear. He wanted to come back to the museum! He said he had not forgotten how much he had enjoyed himself here. He missed being on stage. How's that for human nature? This time, however, he wanted to be paid upfront, but not so much that I couldn't easily afford it. But I reasoned once the man knew what he was worth he would get greedy, not to mention learn English, so I declined. I invest a lot in my properties, Miss Swan, and it always pays to read the fine print.

ANNA   I am not an ignorant savage who cannot read or write English.

BARNUM   That's quite true. In your wildest dreams you could not bring in a quarter of the money that good man brought me. And yet, in his enlightened state, he was no longer useful to me. Let that be / a lesson.

ANNA   I know just how fraudulent this museum is! I know that the Feegee Mermaid is a monkey sewn into the body of a fish. I know that the Woolly Horse is covered with sheep's wool. I know the Missing Link is a black dwarf and Alphonsia and Lucia are really—

BARNUM   Are really what?

ANNA   and I could tell the world.

BARNUM   And if you did, where would that leave us, Miss Anna? I might have to scramble for a month or so to find some new exhibits.

You know there are always more. The publicity wouldn't be a bad thing, of course; whatever gets the public through the doors. Unfortunately, you'd lose all your new-found "friends," and they, well, Miss Anna—I'm sure you've thought of this—they would lose... everything. I don't imagine my Woolly Horse would last long on the streets of New York come summer. You see, I provide employment for creatures who would otherwise be destitute. Now, Miss Anna, have I made myself clear? You stay on my terms or you go on my terms. The first alternative is only open if you behave yourself.

And, Miss Swan, those Albino women, they have put me in a difficult position. I have had a letter from South Carolina. Apparently they are runaway slaves, not free Negroes at all. What a deception they have practised on me. I have no choice but to report them to the authorities. They could be arrested at any time. *(suddenly gentle)* You are not to be involved with them in any way, is that clear? Don't bother checking the contract, Miss Swan.

> ANNA *is staring at the contract.*

You will find I have made provisions for all situations.

SCENE EIGHT

> ANNA *is in* ALPHONSIA's *room.*

ANNA He's going to report you. You both have to leave now!

ALPHONSIA Where to, Anna?

ANNA There are ships leaving for Nova Scotia. I heard from Mr. Jackson. If you sign up quickly you might get on one.

ALPHONSIA I've heard they don't like Negroes much in Nova Scotia either.

ANNA But you would be free!

ALPHONSIA Free to starve? Them winters be some bad up there, I heard they only giving Negroes the very worst land and they be dying like flies.

ANNA You could come with me.

ALPHONSIA	You know there ain't no coach or train gonna let us ride together.
ANNA	We could pretend. You could pretend to be my servant.
ALPHONSIA	And what we do when we get to Nova Scotia and we stop pretending?
ANNA	We can go separately. I can find you when I get back.
ALPHONSIA	You know any Negroes in Nova Scotia, Anna?
ANNA	There was an old man who delivered firewood. I didn't... know him well.
ALPHONSIA	Your mama probably told you to stay away from him.
ANNA	I don't remember.
ALPHONSIA	There's probably a whole lot you don't remember, Anna.
ANNA	We have to do something! You can't let yourselves be arrested.
ALPHONSIA	We could do the play.
ANNA	What!
ALPHONSIA	It's what I really want. Before we leave. Once it's done I'll come with you to Nova Scotia, I promise.
ANNA	You promise?
ALPHONSIA	I need you, Anna, to convince the others.
ANNA	But what about Barnum?
ALPHONSIA	We'll be real quiet and then *boom*.
ANNA	Boom?
ALPHONSIA	Boom. We'll spring it on him. Maybe we can do the same as Mrs. Kemble done.
ANNA	Why, what did she do?
ALPHONSIA	Why, the public loved her so much she had them eatin' out of her hand.

SCENE NINE

*The meeting is called for the rehearsal hall in the basement
of the museum. ANNA, CHANG and ENG, CLOFULLIA, LUCIA,
and ALPHONSIA are all present.*

ANNA　　There have been a number of you who have asked… who
want to do the play again. I must warn you, Barnum has heard
about our rehearsals. I think it will be risky.

LUCIA　　Who told you this?

ANNA　　Barnum himself. He wants to drain the aquarium tanks,
there's to be no more activity in the basement.

ENG　　We could talk to the men who come to drain the tanks, try
and persuade them.

CHANG　　You couldn't persuade your arse to take a fart!

CLOFULLIA　　It's a terrible shame about the whales, poor creatures. Poor
innocents.

CHANG　　A few big fish, what's the problem?

CLOFULLIA　　You have no heart, Mr. Chang. They are God's creatures,
like ourselves.

JACKSON enters.

LUCIA　　Why don't we find out how he heard about the play?

JACKSON　　I told him.

There is a hush.

LUCIA　　There, you see! You think we haven't seen you? Always
watching us after hours, seeing where we go at night.

ENG holds LUCIA back.

ENG　　I think we have to give Mr. Jackson a chance to speak.

LUCIA　　He's done enough speaking. Let's have a confession.

JACKSON　　What are you acc-cusing me of, Miss Lucia?

LUCIA　　Don't you have a file on all of us?

JACKSON　　And what would yours say, Miss Lucia, if I d-did?

LUCIA	You tell me.
JACKSON	Would it say that you go out at night looking for Negro prostitutes? Would it say that you pay out your sister's hard-earned money for the c-c-company of these women, that you pay them extra to strike you, to insult you, to hurt you for c-coming to them at all? Is that what you think I tell Mr. B-Barnum? I'll tell you something. I d-don't think he'd c-care.

LUCIA stands back.

LUCIA	Maybe Charles Dickens got it right, maybe you are the missing link between man and the apes.

There is a silence.

ALPHONSIA	If there be hundreds of people in the gallery, Barnum can't be draining the tank, can he?
LUCIA	What!
ALPHONSIA	If we do the play... in front of / folks.
LUCIA	You'll be laughed off the stage!
ENG	For an audience? Do the play for an audience?
LUCIA	Alphonsia, we got to leave here. You know what's gonna happen.
CHANG	To hell with Barnum. We'll perform in the gallery, to hell with the basement! We are artists.
ENG	The show must go on. The show must go on.
LUCIA	We don't have time to be doing plays!
ENG	What about finding another place? A hall somewhere?
CHANG	I for one don't care about the contract.
CLOFULLIA	That's good for you. I have a child.
ENG	I have several children, Miss Josephine, and it is of the greatest regret to me / that they are not with me.
CHANG	Oh for God's sake, we are talkin' about making art here!
ALPHONSIA	We put a big advertisement in the *New York Times* newspaper on the day, so it's too late for Barnum to cancel. People come

in droves to see what it's all about and we'd tell them it's
a special show to raise money for a new aquarium tank!

LUCIA   Alphonsia!

ANNA   It might work. Mr. Chang, can you prepare the press notes?

ENG   Just don't get drunk.

CHANG   I never get drunk. What shall I say? "Freaks do Shakespeare"?

JACKSON finally speaks up.

JACKSON   No, I will p-prepare the press notes.

There is a hushed silence, a standoff.

ALPHONSIA   I will take Mr. Jackson at his word.

JACKSON   *(with great dignity)* I will d-describe us as Barnum's new
             international acting company. No freaks. Everyone in
             New York will come to see it.

LUCIA   How do we know? We'd have to rehearse every night for at
             least a week. How do we know he won't tell Barnum?

JACKSON   You have my word. I will say nothing to him.

ALPHONSIA   It be all settled then. We gonna invite all of New York City.
             Charge five cents. Rebuild the aquarium tank.

CLOFULLIA   Give the poor creatures a home.

LUCIA   It's insane. You'll lose everything for a few animals who are
             going to die anyway.

ALPHONSIA stares at her.

ENG   It might work!

CHANG   Wake me up when its time to play-act!

JACKSON pulls a paper from his pocket. He reads haltingly.

JACKSON (MALVOLIO)
             Were you not ev'n now with the Countess Olivia?

ALPHONSIA is surprised, but responds calmly.

ALPHONSIA (VIOLA)
             Even now, sir; on a moderate pace I have arriv'd but hither.

JACKSON (MALVOLIO)

> She returns this ring to you, sir. You might have sav'd my pains, to have taken it away yourself…

ALPHONSIA (VIOLA)

> She took no ring of me. I'll none of it.

JACKSON (MALVOLIO)

> Come, sir, you peevishly threw it to her; and her will is, it should be so return'd.

All are amazed that JACKSON no longer stutters.

ANNA   Well done, both of you. Now, let's get on with it. Josephine, your job is costumes. Malvolio needs yellow stockings, you must have something.

CLOFULLIA   I don't / think—

ENG   I have a pair, very nice silk.

ANNA   Excellent, Mr. Eng. You can act as a prompter when you're not in the scene.

LUCIA   This is madness.

She exits. ALPHONSIA follows her.

ENG   *(aside to ANNA)* I heard Barnum is going to send the Lugar women away.

CHANG   Come on, brother!

ANNA   You don't say a word to anyone, Mr. Eng. You either, Mr. Chang. We are all actors now.

SCENE TEN

> *There is the sound of a great crowd of people converging outside the museum. The company is preparing for the play in the gallery. A makeshift stage has been erected stage right. We see the stage from the actors' perspective, from the wings.*
>
> *Titters, nervous conversation.*

ENG   A lot of people are going to have to stand. A lot of people aren't going to make it in at all.

ANNA The doors are locked for another five minutes. Chang, get into costume; you're in the second scene.

CHANG I can't get in costume under these conditions. May I request a dresser?

ENG For forty years I have helped you get dressed. Why should it be any different now?

CHANG Because we are not ourselves now. For the first time in fifty miserable years, I am not your brother, I am Sir Toby Belch.

ENG Oh, for God's sake.

> *JONES and EDWARDS enter through the stage left door carrying hoses.*

CHANG (SIR TOBY)
Out, scab!

ENG I have to protest! This is a private area.

CLOFULLIA Those men, who are they?

ANNA The doors are locked. They must be Barnum's men. Just keep getting ready. Let me deal with them.

EDWARDS We're here to pump out the tanks in the basement. Mr. Barnum's orders.

ANNA I'm sorry. There's a performance going on here tonight. You'll have to come back another time.

EDWARDS Ain't heard nothing about that. We got a job to do.

CLOFULLIA You can't, they die a slow death if you drain the water out.

JONES Calm down, we'll shoot them first.

> *CLOFULLIA looks ill.*

ANNA Shh, Josephine. I'm sorry, you men will have to go. There are people waiting.

EDWARDS Nothing to do with us. Mr. Barnum's orders.

JACKSON Fools.

JONES Hey, I know that little guy! That's the Missing Link. It talks!

> *He grabs JACKSON. There is a struggle.*

JACKSON	Let go of me!
JONES	Not till I get a real good feel for myself. What are you, anyway? Has he got you with sealing wax on your head to make it so pointed? Can you stand straight? What about your hands? Or is it paws? Hey there, let me see them!

JACKSON struggles to free himself.

EDWARDS	Leave it alone! We got work to do!

JONES drops JACKSON.

ALPHONSIA	There be people waiting!
JONES	What's that to us, lady? Hey, you're the white Negro, ain't ya? Now that's no joke. There ought to be a law against that. A white Negro, now that's a sin against God.

There is a pounding at the door downstage.

EDWARDS	Shut up, will ya? Get those hoses.
ANNA	It's the police.
EDWARDS	Christ almighty! The police! That's all we need.

EDWARDS starts yarding in hoses from the side entrance.

ANNA	You can't! There are people waiting, hundreds of people…
EDWARDS	Doors stay locked till we're finished. Just take a few hours. Mr. Barnum's orders.

The pounding intensifies on the huge doors.

	Damn! Sounds like there're gonna break the door down!
CHANG	Stay back! Stay back!

Sound of the door bursting open.

CLOFULLIA	Heavenly God, is half New York City!

ANNA recovers her composure and moves onto the stage as the crowd enters.

ANNA	Please, ladies and gentleman, take your seats. Some of you may have to stand. Tonight we are going to stage a great play by a Mr. William Shakespeare. Some of our actors are new and you may have to be patient with them. At the pause we will pass the hat, not for our own sake, but to build a new home

for the splendid creatures downstairs. We are very grateful to you. And now let the play begin.

> *Sound: a simple lyre and lute Renaissance theme, "Hey Ho the Wind and the Rain." A brief moment of confusion with* EDWARDS *and* JONES. ALPHONSIA *nods to* CLOFULLIA, *who begins.* ENG *prompts from the wings.*

CLOFULLIA (ORSINO)

> If music be the food of love, play on;
> Give me the excess of it, that, surfeiting,
> The appetite may sicken, and so die.
> That strain again, it had a dying fall—

ENG   O...

CLOFULLIA   What?

ENG   O, it came...

CLOFULLIA (ORSINO)

> O, it came—

ENG   O'er my ear...

CLOFULLIA (ORSINO)

> O'er my ear like a sweet sound...
> O, it came o'er my ear like the sweet sound,
> That breathes upon a bank of violets,
> Stealing and giving odour. Enough, no more;
> 'Tis not so sweet now as it was before.

ENG   O...

CLOFULLIA   O...

ENG   O, when mine eyes—

> CLOFULLIA, *concurrently with* EDWARDS.

CLOFULLIA (ORSINO)

> O, when mine eyes...

ENG   Did see Olivia first...

CLOFULLIA (ORSINO)

> ...did see Olivia first,
> Methought she purg'd the air of pestilence!
> That instant was I turn'd into a hart;

And my desires, like fell and cruel hounds,
E'er since pursue me.

EDWARDS grumbles on the sidelines.

EDWARDS   Now we're screwed. Can't get the hoses out.

JONES   Damn freaks are taking over the place.

LADY   *(from the audience)* Please be quiet, I think they are very good.

Music bridge. The scene moves back to the wings.

ANNA is dressed as Olivia, ALPHONSIA as Viola after the shipwreck.

ALPHONSIA   No one see Lucia since last night. She never come back from her walk. Who's gonna play the clown?

ANNA   I… I don't know.

ALPHONSIA   We only got a few scenes, then the whole thing gonna grind to a halt. Just like she'd want it to.

ANNA   Maybe she's at the docks. Alphonsia, you have to go as soon as this is over.

ALPHONSIA   I was looking forward to being a boy. I'll look good as a boy, eh? Good as Lucia?

ANNA   You look good… as either.

ALPHONSIA   Thank you, Anna, whatever happens.

ANNA   You're on!

ALPHONSIA moves on stage.

ALPHONSIA (VIOLA)
I prithee, and I'll pay thee bounteously,
Conceal me what I am, and be my aid
For such disguise as haply shall become
The form of my intent. I'll serve this duke:
Thou shalt present me as an eunuch to him:
It may be worth thy pains; for I can sing
And speak to him in many sorts of music

Her dialogue begins to overlap with JONES and EDWARDS.

> That will allow me very worth his service.
> What else may hap to time I will commit;
> Only shape thou thy silence to my wit.

JONES   She's a pretty one! I'll give her that.

> *He stares at her.*

EDWARDS   Stop gawking, we've got work to do.

> *LUCIA appears in the audience.*

JONES   Look, the other one's over there. I don't like this. All the freaks are loose!

> *Music bridge to* CHANG *and* ENG. ENG *plays Sir Andrew Aguecheek in a blond wig.*

ENG (SIR ANDREW)
> I'll ride home tomorrow, Sir Toby.

CHANG (SIR TOBY)
> *Pourquoi*, my dear knight?

ENG (SIR ANDREW)
> What is *pourquoi*? Do or not do? I would have I had bestowed that time in the tongues that I have in fencing, dancing, and bear-baiting. O, had I but followed the arts!

CHANG (SIR TOBY)
> Then had'st thou had an excellent head of hair?

ENG (SIR ANDREW)
> Why, would that have mended my hair?

> *A huge laugh from the audience.*

GENT   These are very strange actors!

LADY   It's a new company. The actors are from the continent. I read about it in the *Times*.

GENT   Foreigners.

LADY   *(hushed)* Be quiet please or I'll have you put out.

> *LUCIA and JACKSON meet offstage. JACKSON is dressing as Malvolio.*

JACKSON   You're late, Lucia! You had Miss Anna worried.

LUCIA	You'll be recognized.
JACKSON	As what?
LUCIA	You got yourself the part of the jackass…
JACKSON	He be a human jackass.
LUCIA	You never be able to go back. You lose everything, you'll be back on the street!

ANNA interrupts them.

ANNA	Lucia!
LUCIA	I got no costume. I'm not going anywhere.
ANNA	Go on as you are. They're waiting for you.

LUCIA freezes.

JACKSON	That fool is the smartest fellow in the whole play. Doesn't matter what he wears. He sees everything before it happens.
LUCIA	Does he see they all be out of a job soon?
JACKSON	Your mama would be proud, Miss Lucia, to see you out there. She always said you was too smart to be a slave girl.

ALPHONSIA enters as Cesario. She is a stunning boy.

ALPHONSIA   Sister, they's waiting for you.

LUCIA (FESTE)

Well, God give them wisdom that have it; and those that are fools, let them use their talents.

She takes a big breath and goes on stage, leaving JACKSON, ANNA, and ALPHONSIA visibly relieved.

Music bridge. The play moves forward to the cell scene.

Alas, sir, how fell you besides your five wits?

JACKSON (MALVOLIO)

Fool, there was never a man so notoriously abused;
I am as well in my wits, fool, as thou art.

JONES   *(in audience)* Hey, here's the chimp again. See, he's a dwarf, a fake!

LUCIA (FESTE)

But as well? Then you are mad indeed, if you be no better in your wits than a fool.

LADY

Please be quiet! This is a very moving Malvolio. A very interesting character study!

JACKSON (MALVOLIO)

They have here propertied me; keep me in darkness, send ministers to me, asses, and do all they can to face me out of my wits.

BARNUM enters the hall.

LUCIA (FESTE)

Advise you what you say: the minister is here. —*(as SIR TOPAS)* Malvolio, thy wits the heavens restore!

LADY

Why, this fellow is better than Mr. Booth, I assure you!

JACKSON (MALVOLIO)

Sir Topas!

BARNUM

What is going on here? Mr. Jackson! What are you doing up there? Who let these people in?

LUCIA (FESTE)

(as SIR TOPAS) Maintain no words with him, good fellow—

LADY

Can't you see, sir? It's a play. Now please be quiet!

BARNUM

A play! By whom, madam, and at whose behest?

JACKSON (MALVOLIO)

Fool, fool, fool, I say!

LUCIA (FESTE)

Alas, sir, be patient. What say you, sir? I am shent for speaking to you.

LADY

Why, Mr. Barnum's, of course. And a very humanitarian cause, too!

BARNUM bristles.

BARNUM

Madam, I...

LADY And only asking for a donation. I'm going to give him a dollar for all his trouble. I only wish more rich men had his sense of conscience.

The scene continues under with LUCIA *as Feste.*

LUCIA (FESTE)

> I am gone, sir,
> And anon, sir,
> I'll be with you again,
> In a trice,
> Like the old Vice,
> Your need to sustain.

JONES speaks to the crowd concurrently with LUCIA (FESTE).

JONES Hey, he's the Missing Link. He's a counterfeit! A fake!

GENT I knew there was something strange going on.

JONES The one in the monkey cage!

EDWARDS takes JONES aside.

EDWARDS Who asked your opinion, boy? We have a job to do here, Mr. Barnum's orders.

GENT This is just another of Barnum's frauds.

JONES grabs JACKSON from the stage.

JONES Hey, little ape-man! You're not so dumb after all. Why don't you come with us?

EDWARDS Leave the chimp alone. Mr. Barnum will settle with him. Get the hoses through the side, just keep the people back.

> *LUCIA intervenes in an attempt to free JACKSON. A chant of "Fraud! Fraud!" breaks out in the audience along with "On with the play!" from those who want it to continue. The pro-play contingent begin to applaud loudly. JACKSON is pulled into the crowd, who don't seem to know whether to canonize him or tear him apart.*

> *BARNUM huffs his way to the stage.*

BARNUM Ladies and gentlemen. Please, everyone, remain calm. I assure you everyone will be safe… *(aside to ANNA)* Miss Swan, your career in the exhibition gallery is finished. You were fully warned of the consequences of such an act. *(to the audience)* My friends, I cannot say how / sorry—

LADY Bravo, Mr. Barnum, for your wonderful show here tonight. I think it should transfer for an indefinite run in the lecture hall!

BARNUM Why, thank you, madam. I hardly / thought—

GENT Not everyone would be so brave!

LADY I have been moved to tears tonight, sir. And I shall thank you for it for the rest of my life.

> *BARNUM is, for a brief second, lost for words. ANNA takes over, turning to the audience in her biggest, most glowing school-teacher voice.*

ANNA Ladies and gentlemen, it is my honour here tonight to introduce to you not only the great showman you know already but the even greater humanitarian who is too shy to take a bow. Another man might be content to live off the successes of an earlier life, but the man standing before you tonight is not like ordinary men. He takes risks, he understands human nature, and above all he cares deeply for his fellow creatures on this earth. Without him this performance would not have been possible. Ladies and gentlemen, I give you that great promoter of the abolitionist cause, Phineas T. Barnum.

> *There is loud applause mixed with less favourable reviews.*

> *BARNUM is taken aback but responds to the applause.*

BARNUM Well, thank you very much. I had certainly not / intended—

ANNA This performance to raise money for new aquarium tanks is an outstanding demonstration of your generosity and vision. Encouraging the curiosities to take on roles more challenging than their race normally allows was a magnificent gesture on your part, Mr. Barnum. I am only sorry these few patrons lost control. I am sure they can be convinced to settle down for the sake of the others. Perhaps if you offered free tickets for another performance.

> *Applause from the crowd.*

Part of the problem seems to have been overcrowding.

BARNUM   Yes, well that is a good idea, certainly. Ladies and gentlemen, it has always been my intention to educate and entertain. Sometimes we run into difficulty, but we must not lose heart. The American people have always been a source of inspiration to me, as I think we as Americans are to the rest of the world.

> *An explosion is heard from below. From downstairs a voice is heard: "Fire!" The riot turns to confusion, then panic. Cries of "Where are the doors?" and "Get the ladies out!" etc. More confusion.* BARNUM *attempts to maintain control as the curiosities huddle backstage.*

CHANG   The boiler exploded!

CLOFULLIA   The men were sent to drain the tank, maybe they left it too long, it burn up!

BARNUM   Please don't panic! I assure you, ladies and gentlemen, everyone will get out safely.

LUCIA   I heard it's the Sons of Liberty set the fire, they're shooting out the windows.

JACKSON   Someone has to get the animals loose.

LUCIA   No! You can't go down there, leave them.

JACKSON   We c-can't just leave them…

CLOFULLIA   Mr. Barnum not letting wild animals on streets of New York!

JACKSON   They'll suffocate.

> ANNA *grabs him.*

ANNA   You can't go down there.

JACKSON   Let me go!

ANNA   It's too dangerous.

> JACKSON *struggles in her grasp.*

JACKSON   I have to go d-down. They c-can't get out on their own…

> *The panic is building in the audience as they all try to get to the doors.* ANNA *holds* JACKSON *firm to prevent him from descending.*

BARNUM   Please don't panic! I assure you, ladies and gentlemen, the fire brigade has been alerted and will be here as soon as possible. Our men will lead you to the exits. Everyone will leave safely. Any donations tonight will be refunded. This way to the Egress!

> *Another explosion. We hear the cries of distress from the stables and the cages; tigers, elephants, and horses below. BARNUM attempts to reassure the crowd. ALPHONSIA looks at ANNA, who is still holding JACKSON, as billowing smoke comes from the basement. There are screams of panic as the sounds of the fire intensify.*

ALPHONSIA   Let him go, Anna, let him set them free!

ANNA   He'll never come back alive.

> *ALPHONSIA grabs ANNA. ANNA drops JACKSON.*

No, no!

ALPHONSIA   Anna, he be gone. You have go up now, up to the fire escape!

ANNA   What about you? Where are you going?

ALPHONSIA   Quick, Anna.

ANNA   But what about you?

ALPHONSIA   Maybe I make it to Nova Scotia one day. Maybe I find you there. Now go, and be careful. That fire escape's none too strong.

> *The stage is engulfed in flames.*

SCENE ELEVEN

> *All the curiosities except ANNA and BARNUM begin to get out of costume as BARNUM speaks to posterity.*

BARNUM   Anna Swan... classic case of biting the hand that feeds you. If she hadn't been a giantess she would have probably become one of those suffragettes you see nowadays chaining themselves to railings. She was quiet enough in the beginning, but I wasn't fooled; she couldn't leave well enough alone.

I think that's the problem with human entertainment, its just too damned unpredictable.

Michael Chiasson as PT Barnum
photo by Thaddeus Holownia

They said I let the pinhead die, sent him to his death, even.
Could I help it if he was foolhardy enough to run into the
flames? Everyone else got out all right. Anna Swan should have
pulled him out if she was so concerned. God knows we went
to enough trouble, lowering her out of the third floor gallery
window. Bloody elephant of a woman! Those Negro albino
women went somewhere, God knows where. Never saw them
again. What went on in those rooms up there? Do you think
they'd tell me anything? Kept in the dark I was, as always. Not
that I didn't warn them. I don't think the women were any too
healthy, I can tell you that much, not having any men of their
own. I think they were probably up to all sorts of funny things
together and that's where all the trouble started. But I stayed
out of it as long as I could. Didn't want the bad publicity.

BARNUM freezes.

SCENE TWELVE

A bare stage. ANNA *begins to take off her costume and shoe lifts.*

ANNA   I was found at the top of the third-storey staircase, by the fire escape, nearly unconscious. Mr. Eng stood by me as long as he could but was finally persuaded by his brother to escape. I saw a steady stream of people below me, one carried an eagle with no wings, another had a hideous stuffed beast with the face of a snake, several carried birds and sea monsters. God knows where all those things will end up. From somewhere Barnum's men produced a lofty derrick and I was swung over the heads of the crowd to the enthusiastic applause of those below. The fire escape melted beneath me. The fire department when it did arrive was unable to stop the blaze.

In light of these recent tragic events, Mr. Barnum has agreed to release me from the terms of my contract. Given the public outcry over the unsafe conditions that led to the fire, he has been unusually generous.

I have given it a lot of thought and have decided not to return to Nova Scotia. I will be leaving for Europe shortly…

Please tell my brothers and sisters that I think of them often. I enclose a cheque for their welfare. I know you will see it wisely spent.

Dear Mama, I do appreciate your offer to bring me home, but I think it best I stay with this life to which I have become accustomed. In fact, I can say I have begun to take a certain pride in being one of the world's greatest living curiosities.

Your loving daughter,
Anna Swan

I remember seeing cockatoos, parrots, a condor, and two vultures. I remember they were set free to fly over the city.

As actors, they sing Feste's final song, "With a Hey Ho, the Wind and the Rain."

The End

Mary Vingoe has worked in professional Canadian theatre as an actor, playwright, dramaturge, director, teacher, artistic director, and producer. She is a co-founder and past artistic director of Toronto's Nightwood Theatre, co-founder and past co-artistic director of the Ship's Company Theatre in Parrsboro, Nova Scotia, and founding artistic director of the Eastern Front Theatre in Halifax. She is also the inaugural artistic director of the Magnetic North Theatre Festival. Vingoe has directed for major theatres across the country, including the Manitoba Theatre Centre, Prairie Theatre Exchange, Centaur Theatre, Neptune Theatre, Alberta Theatre Projects, and Tarragon Theatre. She has written for radio and television as well as theatre. Her plays include, *Hooligans* with Jan Kudelka, *Holy Ghosters*, *The Herring Gull's Egg*, and *The Company Store*, based on the novel by Sheldon Currie. She has been closely associated as a director and dramaturge with the work of many Canadian playwrights, in particular Wendy Lill, for whom she has directed five world premieres, four of which were nominated for the Governor General's Literary Award for Drama.

Vingoe is the recipient of Halifax's Mayor's Award for Achievement in Theatre, the Robert E. Merritt Award for Achievement in Theatre, a Dora Mavor Moore Award for best production, and the Queen's Jubilee Medal for contribution to the arts. She was recently named winner of the Portia White Award, Nova Scotia' s highest artistic honour.

Mary Vingoe was born in Halifax, Nova Scotia, where she graduated from Dalhousie University. She completed her MA in Drama at the University of Toronto. She is married to composer Paul Cram. They have two daughters, Katharine and Laura.